FLYING HIGH

CANADA

FLYING HIGH

WHITE STAR
PUBLISHERS

632
The low-lying coastal plain of Melville Peninsula, Nunavut, shows foldings from the faulting, uplifting and erosion of the Earth.

633
Baffin Island, Nunavut, is the largest island in Canada and the fifth largest island in the world.

634-635
June in Baffin Island is still a wintry domain of ice and snow.

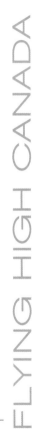

FLYING HIGH CANADA

TEXT

Erin McCloskey

Project Editor

VALERIA MANFERTO DE FABIANIS

Graphic Design

PAOLA PIACCO

Cover
Peyto Lake, in Banff National Park, Alberta.

Back cover
View of Toronto.

1
Horseshoe Falls, a section of Niagara Falls.

2-3
Downtown Vancouver faces onto the ocean.

4-5
A fantasy of color paints this field in Prince Edward Island.

Contents

6-7
Northern British Columbia.

8
The lines of cut wheat in a field in Manitoba.

9
The Mackenzie River, Northwest Territories.

10
A congregation spread far out over the countryside is brought together by this little white-steepled parish church.

11
The Cassiar Mountains, Yukon.

12-13
The famous natural rock arch of Percé Rock, Quebec.

14-15
The Hudson Bay, Manitoba.

16-17
Steep coastal cliffs and deep fjords.

FLYING HIGH CANADA

FLYING HIGH CANADA

Introduction

IN DAYS OF YORE, FROM BRITAIN'S SHORE,

WOLFE THE DAUNTLESS HERO CAME,

AND PLANTED FIRM BRITANNIA'S FLAG

ON CANADA'S FAIR DOMAIN.

HERE MAY IT WAVE, OUR BOAST AND PRIDE,

AND JOIN IN LOVE TOGETHER

THE THISTLE, SHAMROCK, ROSE ENTWINE

THE MAPLE LEAF FOREVER.

(ALEXANDER MUIR), *THE MAPLE LEAF FOREVER*

CONFEDERATION SONG OF 1867

EMBLEMATIC IMAGES OF CANADA, THE THISTLE, SHAMROCK AND ROSE

ARE FOR BRITISH, IRISH AND FRENCH ANCESTRY, WHILE THE MAPLE LEAF,

18
This view looks north over the Rogers Center and the
CN Tower of downtown Toronto, Ontario.

Introduction

ALONG WITH THE BEAVER AND THE CANADA GOOSE, ARE SYMBOLS OF CANADA'S PERSONAL IDENTITY. THE RED AND WHITE FLAG WITH THE SIMPLE MAPLE LEAF IN THE CENTER WAS RAISED FOR THE FIRST TIME IN 1965. PREVIOUSLY IT WAS THE UNION JACK ON THE FLAG; AS A DEMOCRATIC CONSTITUTIONAL MONARCHY, THE QUEEN OF ENGLAND'S FACE IS STILL PRINTED ON THE MONEY. WHEN ONE THINKS OF CANADA, UNDOUBTEDLY IMAGES OF NATURE AND WILDERNESS COME TO MIND. ON THIS LAND GROW SOME OF THE WORLD'S OLDEST AND LARGEST FORESTS, AND OVER IT FLOWS MUCH OF THE WORLD'S FRESH WATER. MOUNTAIN RANGES LORD OVER DEEP VALLEYS AND GREAT INTERLACING RIVERS POUR OVER RAVINES, THROUGH LAKES AND INTO ONE OF THREE OCEANS. THE ARCTIC IS RESPLENDENT WITH ICE CAPS AND GLACIERS AT ONE EXTREME AND THE PRAIRIES BAKE HOT AND DRY IN THE BADLANDS OF THE SOUTHERN LIMITS. SECOND IN SIZE ONLY TO RUSSIA, THE TOTAL AREA OF CANADA IS 9,984,670 SQ. KM (3,854,082 SQ. MI), BUT HOME TO ONLY ABOUT 30 MILLION PEOPLE, APPROXIMATELY THE POPULATION OF CALIFORNIA. MOST OF THE LAND-

Introduction

SCAPE IS HOME TO A DIVERSITY OF WILDLIFE WITHIN THE WILD SPACES EN-
VIED BY MANY OTHER COUNTRIES. THE NORTHERN LIGHTS, OR AURORA BO-
REALIS, IS A SIGHT FOR PRIVILEGED EYES, DANCING AND CRACKLING FOR
SELECT AUDIENCES ONLY. THOUGHT BY EARLY MAN TO BE THE LIGHTS OF
THE GODS AND THE HEAVENS, IT IS HARD NOT TO MAKE THESE ASSOCIA-
TIONS AND FEEL SOME SENSE OF SPIRITUALITY OR INNER PEACE FROM
WATCHING THEM. ANOTHER ICONIC IMAGE IS THAT OF THE ROYAL CANADI-
AN MOUNTED POLICE (RCMP OR "MOUNTIES"). IN SHARP RED JACKETS AND
PATROLLING ON HORSEBACK, THE MOUNTIES ARE THE FEDERAL POLICE
BUT THEY ALSO PUT ON A GOOD SHOW PERFORMING THE MUSICAL RIDE,
AN IMPRESSIVE DRESSAGE EVENT WITH THE ENTOURAGE RIDING IN FOR-
MATION IN KALEIDOSCOPIC PATTERNS TO DEMONSTRATE THEIR HIGH LEV-
EL OF EQUESTRIAN SKILL. THE FIRST NATIONS ARE THE WAKASHAN, SALIS-
HAN, TSIMWHIAN, TLINGIT, HAIDAN, ATHAPASKAN (TAIGA-ATHAPASKAN ANCES-
TORS OF TODAY'S SLAVEY, MOUNTAIN DENE AND GWICH'IN PEOPLES),
KOOTENAIAN, ALGONQUIAN, SIOUIAN, IROQUOIAN, ESKALEUT AND BEOTHUK,

Introduction

WITH 53 LANGUAGES AMONGST THEM. THE FIRST EUROPEANS WERE THE BRITISH AND FRENCH, WHO REMAIN TODAY THE MAJORITY DEMOGRAPHIC: BRITISH DESCENT 28% AND FRENCH DESCENT 23%. THE NUMBER OF ITALIAN-CANADIANS IS THREE PERCENT, HIGHER THAN ABORIGINAL (TWO PERCENT) AND THE NEXT SIGNIFICANT CULTURAL GROUPS INCLUDE THE GERMAN, UKRAINIAN, DUTCH, GREEK, POLISH, CHINESE, JAPANESE AND ICELANDIC, AND EACH OF THESE GROUPS HAS DENSE POCKETS IN VARIOUS PARTS OF THE COUNTRY. FOR EXAMPLE, THE ICELANDIC PEOPLE SETTLED IN LARGE NUMBERS AROUND LAKE WINNIPEG; THE FIRST OLYMPIC GOLD MEDAL IN HOCKEY, THE COUNTRY'S NATIONAL SPORT, WAS WON BY A TEAM THAT WAS ALL BUT ONE ICELANDIC. CANADA HAS TEN PROVINCES AND THREE TERRITORIES. THE MARITIMES IS THE COLLOQUIAL NAME FONDLY GIVEN TO THE ATLANTIC PROVINCES. NOVA SCOTIA'S HISTORY ABOUNDS IN PIRATE STORIES FROM THIS ISLAND'S LEGENDARY PAST, SUCH AS THAT OF CAPTAIN KIDD, WHOSE REPUTEDLY UNCLAIMED TREASURE IS STILL BURIED HERE. THE MUSIC FROM NOVA SCOTIA'S CAPE BRETON ISLAND CAN BE

Introduction

HEARD ACROSS THE WATERS; THE ENTIRE ISLAND SEEMS TO KNOW HOW TO PLAY THE FIDDLE OR STEP DANCE. POTATO FIELDS REACH FROM THE BRICK-RED SOILS DOWN TO THE WHITE SANDY SHORES OF PRINCE EDWARD ISLAND. THE CONFEDERATION MET HERE IN 1864 TO ESTABLISH CANADA AND CONFEDERATION BRIDGE NOW CONNECTS THE ISLAND TO THE FORESTED SHORES OF NEW BRUNSWICK; 8 MI (12.9 KM) LONG, THE BRIDGE IS THE LONGEST OVER ICE-COVERED WATERS IN THE WORLD. NORTH OF THE GULF OF ST. LAWRENCE IS THE FOURTH ATLANTIC PROVINCE OF NEWFOUNDLAND AND LABRADOR, WHICH DID NOT JOIN CANADA UNTIL 1899. SOFT GREEN MOUNTAINS AND THE COLORFULLY PAINTED HOUSES OF THE FISHING VILLAGES ARE CHARACTERISTIC OF THIS PROVINCE. QUEBEC IS SEEMINGLY EUROPEAN, AND ITS ELEGANT AND BEAUTIFUL ARCHITECTURE IS THE OLDEST IN THE COUNTRY. THOUGH CANADA IS OFFICIALLY BILINGUAL, ENGLISH AND FRENCH, IN PRACTICE, THE LATTER IS MOSTLY SPOKEN IN QUEBEC, THE LARGEST FRENCH-SPEAKING POPULATION OUTSIDE OF FRANCE. QUEBEC CAME UNDER

Introduction

BRITISH CONTROL BUT NEVER GAVE UP ITS CULTURE; FRENCH IS STILL SPOKEN MORE THAN 245 YEARS LATER. ONTARIO IS THE MOST POPULATED PROVINCE WITH THE LARGE CITY OF TORONTO AND THE NATION'S CAPITAL OTTAWA. TORONTO IS THE CULTURAL HUB WHERE DOZENS OF LANGUAGES ARE HEARD IN THE STREETS. TORONTO SUPPORTS OVER SEVENTY FOREIGN-LANGUAGE NEWSPAPERS AND MUNICIPAL NOTICES ARE ROUTINELY PRINTED IN SIX LANGUAGES: ENGLISH, FRENCH, CHINESE, ITALIAN, GREEK, PORTUGUESE. THE CHINESE COMMUNITY IS THE LARGEST IN NORTH AMERICA OUTSIDE SAN FRANCISCO. THE PRAIRIE PROVINCES ARE MANITOBA, SASKATCHEWAN AND ALBERTA. MANITOBA IS GOLDEN WITH WHEAT AND SUNFLOWERS IN THE SOUTH AND GREEN WITH BOREAL FOREST IN THE NORTH. ITS CAPITAL OF WINNIPEG STRONGLY SUPPORTS THE ARTS AND THE NORTHERN TOWNS SUCH AS CHURCHILL AND FLIN FLON EXPERIENCE POLAR BEARS AND SUCH COLD TEMPERATURES IN THE WINTER THAT WATER PIPES ARE ABOVE GROUND AND SURROUNDED BY LONG INSULATED WOODEN BOXES TO PREVENT FREEZING. ONCE SEEING THE

Introduction

ENDLESS SKIES OF THE FLAT SASKATCHEWAN PRAIRIES ALL OTHER PLACES SEEM SMALL. THE RCMP WAS ESTABLISHED IN SASKATCHEWAN TO POLICE THE UNRULY CANADIAN WILD WEST AND THE TRAINING ACADEMY IS STILL BASED IN THE CITY OF REGINA. ALBERTA'S GREAT PARKS, SUCH AS WOOD BUFFALO NATIONAL PARK AND THE MOUNTAIN PARKS OF JASPER, BANFF AND WATERTON NATIONAL PARKS AND MANY PROVINCIAL PARKS, STRIVE TO PROTECT THE DIVERSE ECOLOGY. THE CALGARY STAMPEDE HOLDS ITS AN-NUAL HOEDOWNS AND RODEOS AND DRUMHELLER AND DINOSAUR PROVINCIAL PARK ARE RICH IN FOSSILS. THE THREE NORTHERN TERRITO-RIES ARE THE YUKON, NORTHWEST TERRITORIES AND THE NEWLY FORMED NUNAVUT (1999), WHICH IS FIVE TIMES THE SIZE OF CALIFORNIA, 80% INUIT AND THE LARGEST NATIVE LAND CLAIM IN CANADIAN HISTORY. THE NORTH-WEST TERRITORIES ARE LARGELY TUNDRA, SPARSELY POPULATED BY PEO-PLE BUT HOME TO MUSK OXEN AND TUNDRA WOLVES. THE YUKON IS WHERE THE 1898 KLONDIKE GOLD RUSH OCCURRED AND WHERE PEOPLE STILL PAN FOR GOLD NUGGETS IN THE RIVERS. TO LINK THIS VAST EXPANSE,

FLYING HIGH CANADA

26
The pure white iceberg reflects the soft light of the moon.

28-29
The last stalks of this Saskatchewan wheat field are about to be cut.

THE BUILDING OF THE FIRST TRANSCONTINENTAL RAILWAY WAS INAUGU-
RATED BY THE CANADIAN PACIFIC RAILWAY IN 1885. BRITISH COLUMBIA HAS
BOTH LARGE COSMOPOLITAN CITIES, SUCH AS VANCOUVER, A HUB FOR
THE ARTS AND BUSINESS, AND SMALL TOWNS WHERE SOME CANADIANS
ARE CHOOSING TO LIVE "OFF THE GRID" IN REMOTE LOCATIONS IN THE
MOUNTAINS OR ON THE PACIFIC ISLANDS, WITH MORE ENCOUNTERS WITH
ANIMAL NEIGHBORS THAN THE HUMAN SORT. GLOBALLY RECOGNIZED
FOR HIGH QUALITY OF LIFE, WITH A STABLE, PROGRESSIVE GOVERNMENT
AND HEALTHY ECONOMY, NUMEROUS PARKS AND THIRTEEN WORLD HER-
ITAGE SITES, EIGHT OF WHICH ARE NATURAL, THE UNITED NATIONS
RANKED CANADA THE BEST COUNTRY IN THE WORLD TO LIVE FOR EIGHT
CONSECUTIVE YEARS.

30-31
The Shepody River flows into Shepody Bay.

32-33
A river winds through the lush green summer forests in New Brunswick.

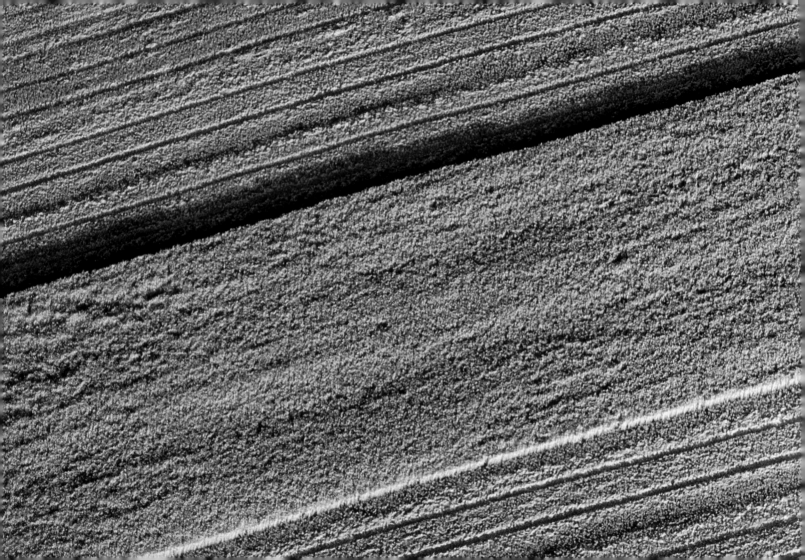

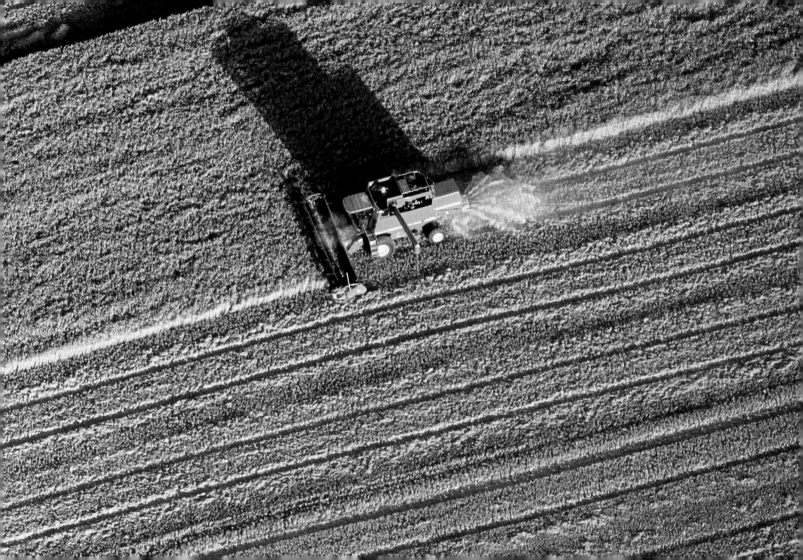

ANCIENT HORIZONS
FLYING HIGH

FLYING HIGH CANADA

35
Blackcomb Mountain, British Columbia (left); Whister Valley,
British Columbia (right).

Only the mountain has lived long enough to listen objectively to the howl of a wolf.

(Aldo Leopold), *Thinking Like a Mountain*

Wolves, grizzlies and cougars still roam the western Canadian mountains, the Canadian Cordillera, treading upon the 1.5-billion-year-old rocks. This sedimentary rock was once at the bottom of the ocean and was relatively undisturbed allowing it to build layers of sediment up to 20 km (12 mi) thick until, being the leading edge of the great Continental tectonic plate, it collided with the Pacific tectonic plate. The result was the pushing up of the ocean floor like the crumpling of a carpet pushed against a wall, and thus explains the existence of coral, clam and oyster fossils on the tops of mountain peaks, 3000 m (9842 ft)

above the ocean shore. Mountain building began here 140 million years ago and ended about 45 million years ago but the two plates have continued to butt heads ever since, causing the famous west coast earthquakes.

The Rocky Mountains, "the Rockies," extend north to the Mackenzie and Selwynn Mountains in the Yukon and south into the United States. The highest point in Canada's Rockies is Mt. Robson at 3450 m (11,319 ft) above sea level, the lowest point at 305 m (1000 ft) at the confluence of the Liard and Toad rivers. The Rockies slope east into the Alberta Foothills, which are part of a critical migratory corridor for wide-ranging species such as the grizzly and an important wildlife refuge. The montane is a term to define the lower valleys on the

36
Mount Robson, 3954 m (12,973 ft), is the highest mountain
in the Canadian Rockies.

39

Mount MacKenzie in the Kootenay's Rainbow Range, one of
the Coastal Ranges in British Columbia, has an elevation
of 2146 m (7041 ft).

eastern slopes and foothills of the Rockies where deer, elk and other ungulates find essential winter habitat, and thus wolves and cougars also find prey in winter. The valleys are more sheltered and milder of climate and thus important refuges. It is a small prized area, unfortunately also prized by humans who have chosen to develop golf courses on the smooth valley floors...and then wonder why the course is covered in elk!

The internationally acclaimed National Mountain Parks of Jasper, Banff, Yoho, Kootenay and Waterton Lakes receive millions of visitors every year, winter and summer, from all over the world to hike, ski, camp and explore. It is a challenging management situation to balance the draw of tourism to this spectacular area and not overdevelop and over-impact this sensitive ecological area. Along the western edge of the Rockies is the Rocky Mountain Trench, a massive 45-million-year-old gorge that is visible from space. Rising up again on the east side of the trench are the Columbia Moun-

tains, which then descend west into the bountiful orchards of the Okanagan and the East Kootenay valleys in British Columbia. The Rockies were known to the aboriginal peoples as the "shining mountains," perhaps alluding to the massive glaciers glinting on its flanks. The Coast Mountains are still glaciated rising to well over 2440 m (8000 ft) and popping up again as the Vancouver Island Mountains, which seldom exceed 2130 m (7000 ft) but they rise abruptly from the shoreline, a stunning scene repeated along much of Canada's coast but in few other places on Earth.

The western Coast Mountains have a pronounced impact on the local climate, catching precipitation from the ocean and dropping it down onto the rainforest and above 1070 m (3500 ft) in winter, creating abundant snow; the excessively athletic can opt to jump in a kayak and don skis on the same day. The Coast Mountains create a great rainshadow that keeps the interior B.C. valleys the driest parts of the province followed by another

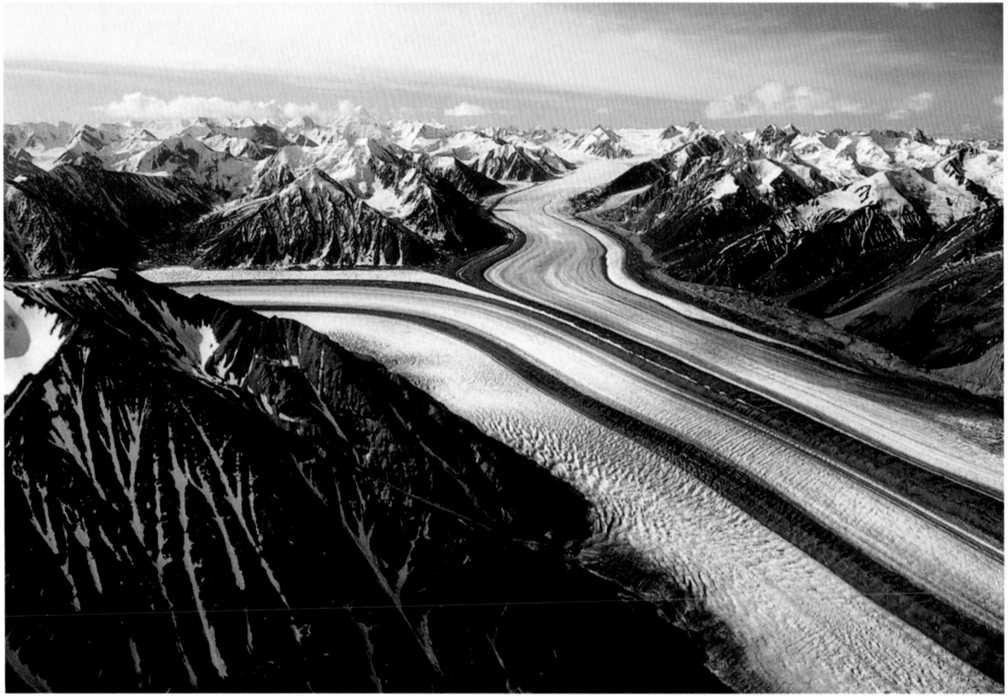

Looking like giant ice freeways, glaciers are all affected by
gravity and journeying to the lowest elevations often merge with
other glaciers from separate ice fields.

rainbelt that hits the subsequent mountain ranges to the east, which are all drier on their eastern slopes. The Canadian Shield is the great granite heart of the center of the country upon which the Great Plains lie mostly flat except for a hiccup called the Cypress Hills. Rising 600 m (1950 ft) above the surrounding ranch land, the Cypress Hills are the highest point of land between the Rockies and Labrador and are crowned with majestic lodgepole pines. Reaching the eastern seaboard, mountains are again encountered. The Atlantic Maritime peninsulas and islands form the northeastern limit of this Appalachian Mountain chain that runs south to Alabama. The highest point, Mount Carleton in New Brunswick, reaches 807 m (2648 ft).

The Arctic Cordillera, or Northeast Seaboard Range, or sometimes referred to as the Arctic Rockies, runs some 2000 km (1243 mi) along the northeastern edge of Nunavut, most of Labrador, and throughout the archipelago along eastern Baffin Island and the Devon, Ellesmere and Bylot islands. Some of Canada's highest mountain peaks are in the Arctic Cordillera, some exceeding 2 km (1.25 mi) in height, and the ten highest are all higher than 2347 m (7700 ft), but few people have ever seen them. The highest peak is Barbeau Peak (2616 m/8583 ft) on Ellesmere Island in Nunavut's Quttinirpaaq National Park.

High basalt faces stare into the brunt of arctic winds, keeping a stoic expression. Shattered by centuries of frost, their crowns are jagged and appear like cathedral pinnacles. Flying above these mountains, the clear pure air makes them appear startling close as the bare rocky peaks reach out against the crystalline white landscape. The climate is desert-like and few animals are adapted to such cold, dry conditions, such as resilient cliff nesting birds. Most dialogues with the mountains here are made with the howling polar winds; indeed, these conversations have been ongoing since time immemorial.

42
The glaciated Selwyn Mountains are the second highest range in the Yukon with peaks up to 2515 m (8250 ft) above sea level, straddling the southern with the Northwest Territories.

43
Broad high plateaus, breathtaking valleys and rolling uplands of dense boreal forest above river valleys and extensive areas of alpine tundra characterize these mountain ranges.

44-45

Mount Logan, in Yukon's St. Elias Mountains, is the highest mountain in Canada at 5959 m (19,550 ft) and is apparently still rising owing to the ongoing tectonic uplifting. It's estimated to have the largest base circumference of any mountain on Earth.

46-47

The western boundary of the Nahanni National Park Reserve, Yukon, is formed by the glacier-covered Selwyn range and the aptly named Ragged Range of igneous rock of the Mackenzie Mountains.

FLYING HIGH CANADA

49
Old Crow Flats in the northern Yukon is an important habitat for waterfowl and mammals, especially the Porcupine caribou that migrate here in spring and late fall in huge numbers and upon which the Gwich'in people are dependent for food and clothing.

50

Southern Yukon is dominated by the Kluane icefields in Kluane National Park and Reserve.

51

The largest non-polar icefields in the world and eight of Canada's ten highest mountains are found within Kluane National Park and Reserve.

52-53

The Yukon is famous for its ice and snow, world-class glaciers and non-polar icefields.

54-55
The basalt peaks of the Tombstone Range have been shattered into arêtes, hornes and sheer faces, giving its characteristic rugged appearance. Tombstone Mountain is the centerpiece of this spiky tiara.

FLYING HIGH CANADA

56

Within the ragged mountains of the Backbone Range of the Selwyn Mountains are sharp ridges and peaks; one small cluster of peaks and walls is called the Cirque of the Unclimbables.

57

The Selwyn Mountains are part of the Mackenzie Mountains of the Northwest Territories and Yukon.

58

The layers of time and geology are evident in this peak in the Sentinel Range, British Columbia. Three-quarters of this province are mountainous.

59

A long and profound glacial valley along the Sentinel Range of British Columbia. The deepest recession of this valley forms a lake, deep and blue. Three mountain ranges, the Rockies, Coast and Vancouver Island, serrate much of the landscape of B.C. into peaks, plateaus and valleys.

60-61

Vancouverites that love hiking and mountian climbing are fortunate to reside at the feet of the Coast Mountians where they can readily participate in their favorite pastimes. From these peaks called The Lions, we can see the city of Vancouver along the shores of the Pacific Ocean.

62

Garibaldi Provincial Park in British Columbia is a treasured destination for skiers and mountain climbers. Garibaldi Mountain is a 2678 m (8786 ft) high stratovolcano.

63

With an area of over 1950 sq. km (753 sq. mi), Garibaldi Provincial Park is comprised of numerous snow-capped mountains and glacier-fed alpine lakes and streams.

64

The Alaska Panhandle dips down into British Columbia and borders the Canadian territories of Yukon and the Northwest Territories in the north.

65

Encompassing British Columbia's Northern Rocky Mountains is the largest roadless landscape in North America south of the 60th parallel — an area the size of Switzerland with no road access.

66
Montane is a term to describe the productive sheltered mountain valleys.

67
Yoho National Park is filled with glacier lakes, waterfalls, snow-topped mountains, forests, and valleys.

68-69
The Meade Glacier lies on the frozen border between British Columbia and Alaska.

70-71

Glaciers dominate the passes in the Chilkoot Range in British Columbia; this is the southernmost extent of its range, which is mostly in the Yukon and reaches into Alaska. The Chilkoot Pass was the route the prospectors took on their way to the Klondike Gold Rush.

72
The snow at the feet of Mount Outram persists year-round. The Howse River and Glacier Lake, the largest lake in Banff National Park, are the two main valleys flanking this mountain.

73
Many small towns sit nestled in the Canadian mountains, such as Hope, B.C., in the Fraser River Canyon.

74

Whistler Mountain, was originally called London Mountain owing to the heavy rain and fog on its flanks.

75

Blackcomb Mountain is 2436 m (7992 ft) high. Its peaks challenge skiers

78
In the summer months, Whistler B.C.'s slopes lend themselves to mountain bikers and hikers.

79
High precipitation in Whistler B.C. results in famously rich powder, desired by skiers.

80
Jasper National Park in the Canadian Rocky Mountains encompasses some of the most important montane habitat, highest peaks and significant glaciers in the country.

81
The Mistaya River valley (Alberta) has a wide floodplain of glacier melt-water that creates wet meadows and fosters abundant spruce forest.

82

Glacier Lakes in Banff National Park, Alberta, are famously beautiful, and famously cold.

83

Peyto Lake, in Banff National Park, Alberta, takes on a stunning blue color from what is called glacier flour: a fine powder created by Peyto glacier scraping over the bedrock, which is then flushed into the lake by meltwater.

84

The tiny hamlet of Lake Louise is in the heart of Banff National Park, a UNESCO World Heritage Site. The majestic Fairmont Chateau Lake Louise nestled at the foot of the lake was originally built in 1890.

85

Upper Waterfowl Lake (Alberta) and the steep cliffs of Mount Chephren. The lower part of the mountain is made of reddish and pinkish quartzites of Lower Cambrian age. The higher levels are made of younger grey limestones. Mount Chephren is a landmark in the Mistaya Valley.

86

The Columbia Icefield at the boundary of Banff and Jasper National Parks, Alberta, holds one of the largest accumulations of ice and snow south of the Arctic Circle. It feeds eight major glaciers as well as rivers that pour into the Arctic, Atlantic and Pacific oceans.

87

Jasper National Park was established in 1907 after the Grand Trunk Pacific Railway line through the Yellowhead Pass was erected. It is the largest national park in the Canadian Rockies.

88

The Highwood Range, just one of the many ranges in the Canadian Rockies, takes on a characteristic backbone structure. Western slopes are greener owing to higher precipitation.

89
The Bow Range is one of the most spectacular in Banff National Park with peaks
visible from Lake Louise.

90-91
Kananaskis country, Alberta, is in the
foothills of the Rockies, a gentle yet intriguing landscape that romantically
lends itself to exploration by horseback.

92
Nature's masonry talents created this fortress. Castle Mountain is a regal formation in Alberta.

93
The backbone of Bowe Range, Alberta.

94-95
Jasper National Park, Alberta, has a history of fur traders, mountaineers, prospectors, railroad surveyors and geologists who explored these daunting and inspiring mountains.

96

The Athabasca Glacier, Miette Hotsprings, Sunwapta and Athabasca Falls, Mount Edith Cavell's impressive glaciers and the Maligne Canyon are all within Jasper National Park, Alberta.

98
The tips of mountains rise above the clouds in Jasper National Park, Alberta.

99
Explorers and adventurers take up the challenge to climb, cross and navigate a world that only alpine wildlife is adapted to.

100

Auyuittuq Park, Nunavut territory, has a native name that means "land that never melts." The Arctic Circle passes through the park, marked by an Inuit trail marker figurine, called an inukshuk.

101

The Penny Ice Cap on Baffin Island, Nunavut, is theorized to be the original ice formation of the last ice age. It covers over 5000 sq. km (2200 sq. mi).

102
The flat-topped Mount Asgard in Auyuit-tuq Park, Nunavut, is surrounded by gla-ciers.

103
The characteristic flat-top of Mount As-gard. Hiking and climbing is only possi-ble during a short time each year late in the summer.

104
Parc du Mont Sainte-Anne (Quebec) is a provincial park and popular leisure area in the Laurentian Mountains.

105
Mont Tremblant supports skiing and snowboarding in winter and hiking in the summer at the popular resort in the Laurentian Mountains of Quebec.

106

Ungava Peninsula in Labrador's Torngot Mountains.

107

The Torngot Mountains include the highest peaks in continental eastern North America but more stunning are the bold landscape features created by the glaciers and continental shifting.

108-109

On the exposed coastal walls in the Torngot Mountains the folding of the eastern edge of the Canadian Shield can be seen. Four-billion-year-old granite was pushed upwards to form the elevated land mass now called Labrador.

MAPLE LEAVES AND PINE CONES

FLYING HIGH

FLYING HIGH CANADA

Gros Morne, Newfoundland (left); forests of red maples
in Quebec (right).

Of the eloquent, calm Old Woods!
While the thoughtless dream
Of some baseless theme,
Here we can stroll,
With exalted soul,
Through the eloquent, calm Old Woods.

(Charles Sangster), *The Fine Old Woods*

When strolling within old forest groves, it is hard not to feel surrounded by wise elders, that the old trees hold secrets to our history that we shall never know. We aspire to their serenity and respect them instinctually. The cool moss-covered misty temperate rainforest of Canada's west coast is the oldest on earth and within its ancient groves are some of the oldest trees on the planet, the oldest living species on the planet.

Western red cedar commonly lives 800 years but can surpass 1300, aging to almost 1500; Douglas fir can live ten or twelve centuries; yellow cedar may have the corner on .longevity with a felled tree on record having revealed 1835 annual growth rings. This rainforest has more than twice the biomass per hectare than the tropical rainforests of Asia and South America, and has larger trees. A dozen people would need to hug the trunk of a western red cedar and reach fingertip to fingertip to encircle it; the largest on record has a trunk circumference of 19 m (62 ft) and 59 m (194 ft) tall.

The Douglas fir is typically the highest of the canopy and therefore champions the area it can cover as well. It grows about 73.8 m (242 ft) in height, but the record breaker of its species is 83 m (272 ft) tall.

112
Several important rivers wind their way through the thick boreal
forest that cloaks more than half of Yukon's area.

FLYING HIGH CANADA

The tallest known western hemlock is on Vancouver Island measuring 75.6 m (248 ft).

The Carmanah Giant is Canada's tallest tree and the world's tallest Sitka spruce at 96 m (314 ft). The overall diversity of B.C.'s forests is the highest on the continent. B.C.'s rarest forest, considered one of the most endangered ecosystems in North America, is the arbutus and Garry oak woodland in the dry rainshadow climate of the Gulf Islands and Saanich Peninsula. Records are set, too, by the boreal forest: it is the largest, coldest and slowest-growing forest in Canada. It is circumpolar, the northernmost, highest altitude forest and covered in snow eight months of the year. Mostly coniferous, the thick boughs of pine, spruce, fir and tamarack provide shelter to wildlife and a rich greenery to the white Canadian winter. This forest forms a continent-wide band spanning 10° of latitude and extending in a wide arc from Newfoundland to Alaska; it is bounded by Aspen Parkland (aspen and poplars transitioning to grassland) to the south, and the subarctic northern taiga, which stretches from Labrador to Alaska and from Siberia to Scandinavia. The Russian term taiga refers to the broad ecotone of subarctic forest and tundra in North America and Eurasia; it is the "land of little sticks" where the spruce and firs become stunted or *krummholz*, a German word meaning crooked wood. To those with imagination, the taiga forest is the fantastical domain of the elfin people — trees rarely exceed the height of a child, due to the persistent winds, low temperatures and limited precipitation. Forest fires often destroy large areas of taiga but have a diversifying effect on the landscape with new growth and wildlife habitat. The area is boggy and the ever-shifting, freezing and thawing soils often cause the trees to tip in random directions, giving the impression of a drunken forest.

Sugar maple, yellow birch, sycamores, sweetgum, oaks, magnolias, beech and hickories foliate the diversity of the mixed-wood Acadian forests in the east. A delirium of autumn colors — red, yellow,

117
The mixed-wood Acadian forests are famous for their autumn
colors. This example is from Prince Edward Island.

orange and purple — with a complexity of hues paint a masterpiece canopy. Boasting the bright red leaves is the sweet sugar maple whose celebrated sap is refined into an amber syrup and poured onto pancakes across the country; maple syrup is probably the most iconic condiment of Canada. The eastern hemlock forests mix white pine, red pine and yellow birch, which sound colorful but are actually mostly green, the transition between the Acadian forest and the boreal.

For centuries Canadians have been reliant on the forest; totemic west coast cultures carved their canoes from the great trees and thus sustained a maritime livelihood; the Plains Indians used the long strait conifer trunks for travois and teepee poles, and later the settlers used these same trees to build lodges, thus christening these trees lodgepole pines.

A sugary stickiness binds the locals to the fruit trees of British Columbia's valleys and the sugar-sweet maples in Acadia; the homes of the early pi-

oneers and the increasing populations of today are mostly wood-framed; pulp, paper and timber industries are critical to Canada's resource-based economy. These extractive industries have lent their way to greed and industrialization, which has resulted in fewer jobs but more forest exploitation, low stumpage fees and the importation of polluting pulpmills banned in more developed countries. Centuries of forestry have left few pockets of old-growth in any of Canada's forests.

Today, forests are predominantly secondary and tertiary growth on old clear-cuts. B.C.'s Bowron Valley clearcut at its zenith was so vast that it could be seen from outer space. It remains the world's largest contiguous clearcut. On the west coast it was the little-known Marbled Murrelet and the now-infamous spotted owl that managed to slow the rate of cutting of the ancient coastal groves, and with continued awareness, exploitative logging will, hopefully, subside, and allow future generations to stroll through the calm old woods.

FLYING HIGH CANADA

118
The mist enwrapped treetops of this piece of forest along the Coquihalla Highway, British Columbia, hide from view the incredible biodiversity.

119
The autumn colors are starting to show in the forest along Coquihalla Highway. The boreal has a great proportion of coniferous trees, which will keep the forest green throughout the winter.

120

The beauty of an intact section of forest along the British Columbia coastline. Incredible biodiversity and a great "lung" of the Earth is represented by this photo. This intricate ecological system is vital to the health of the planet — the water, air and all living things.

121

Cut logs line the logging roads, near Prince George, B. C., in this clear cut (two additional ones are in the background). These small cuts are part of a much larger problem in British Columbia.

FLYING HIGH CANADA

123
Selective logging in British Columbia allows the integrity of the forest to survive by leaving most of the ecology intact and allowing for natural succession to occur.

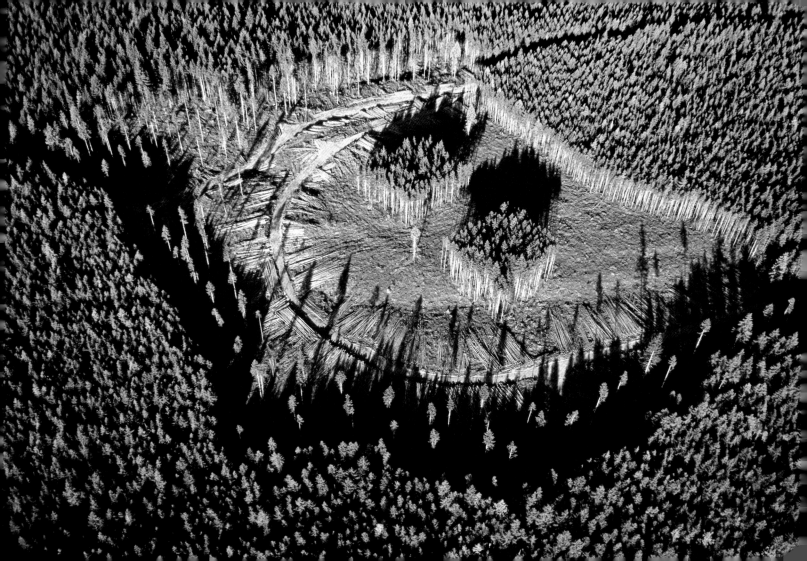

124-125
There are stark lines of transition where forest meet agricultural zones, such as this example in Saskatchewan.

FLYING HIGH CANADA

127
Frosty evergreens are surrounded by luxurious blankets of snow in Saskatchewan.

128-129
A forest fire has occurred here. Fire is a natural and valuable stage in the lifecycle of a forest, keeping it healthy, promoting new growth and clearing excessive brush.

130
Trees can be admirably opportunistic, finding a way to thrive even on the steep cliffs west of Lake Superior, Ontario.

132

Glaciers carved out the Elora Gorge in Rockwood, Ontario. The Eramosa River flows through the forest and ancient sinkholes are left from when the river was much wider.

133

The beautiful mixed-wood forest continues to grow in splendor along the Grand River, Ontario, though further afield, the forest has been replaced by agriculture.

134-135

In the early 17th century, the only way for people to cross these dense woods was by following the passageways made by the Mattawa River, Ontario, which provided an important canoe route for the fur trade.

136
Established in 1971, the Mastigouche Wildlife Reserve was and still is a secluded area favored by hunters and fishermen.

137
Drawn by giant forests and the promise of excellent wood production,
English, Irish and Scottish immigrants were the first to settle in this terri-
tory that is now within Jacques Cartier Park in Quebec.

138
Lines of trees, water and meadow make interesting and colorful patterns in Quebec.

139
Green spruce and pines, yellow poplar, dark red oak and scarlet maple make the forest in fall spectacular in Quebec.

140
A UNESCO biosphere reserve, Charlevoix, Quebec, owes its magnificent geography to a 15-billion-ton meteorite that fell to earth 350 million years ago. The St. Lawrence river runs through the hinterland.

141
Water courses in a difficult path through the bog in Quebec.

142
Some Canadians find seclusion along lakeshores surrounded by deep forests, such as at this quiet lakeside cottage in Quebec.

143
Mastigouche Wildlife Reserve is resplendent with winding rivers and hundreds of lakes which, along with the surrounding forests, provide habitats for fish, mammals and birds.

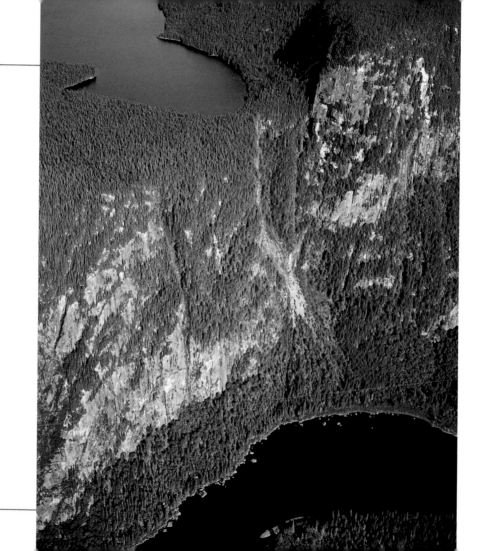

144 and 145

The steep and rugged ground that these forests have carpeted in Quebec protects them from being harvested. Difficulty in accessing this wilderness has kept it quite untouched. The Moisie River provides clean and unspoiled habitat for salmon. The Hanging Lake majestically crowns the mountains, like a goblet held up to the skies.

146 and 147

Gros Morne National Park of Canada was designated a UNESCO World Heritage Site in 1987 and encompasses 1805 sq km (697 sq mi) in the Bonne Bay region of western Newfoundland. It protects the Western Newfoundland Forest, the Long Range Barrens and the Northern Peninsula Forest.

FLYING HIGH CANADA

149
Elk (*Cervus elephus*) are widely dispersed across the forested regions of Canada's provinces, from Vancouver Island all the way to Newfoundland, where this small herd is traversing a forest clearing. Elk are also raised domestically in Canada for their meat, antler felt and hides.

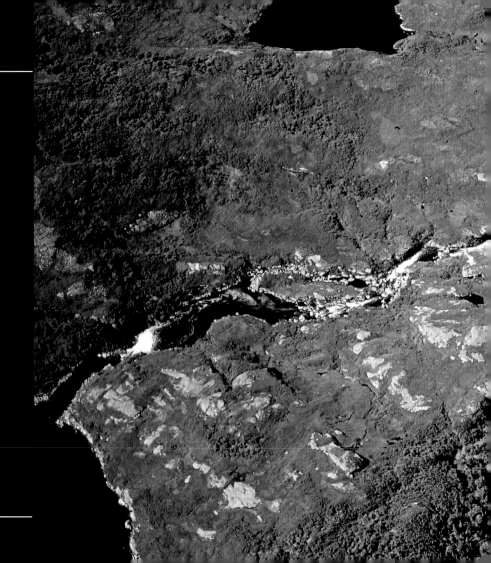

150-151
Gros Morne National Park of Canada is an area of great natural beauty with a rich variety of scenery, wildlife and recreational activities.

152

In 1603, Pierre Dugua, Sieur de Mons, Lieutenant General of "La Cadie" (Acadie) searched for a suitable site for settlement and discovered what he named Saint Croix Island. He tried to establish a year-round French settlement on this now International Historic Site, an event that symbolizes the founding of Acadie.

153

Minister's Island is named after the loyalist Anglican minister, Reverend Samuel Andrews who settled on the island in 1786.

154-155
New Brunswick forest carpets the hillsides with deciduous trees that will turn spectacular colors in fall and conifers that will stay green year round.

156
The autumn colors are just beginning to appear in New Brunswick; soon
the forest will be more red than green.

157
Trees feel the seasons at varying moments in time; this maple is in full
blush while the surrounding trees are mainly green or completely bare.
Deadwood and leaves will soon fall into the water adding nutrients.

158

Squares of pastureland for sheep and cattle are cut out of the forest of Prince Edward Island. Farm communities are considered by many to be the backbone of the Island's culture.

160
Cabins are sprinkled along the shores of Trout River on Prince Edward Island's north shore. Fishing and boating as well as strolling through the lovely woods are popular pastimes here.

161
Pass a peaceful day golfing on Prince Edward Island.

162
The styles of farmhouses in Nova Scotia reflect the national origins of the English, Irish, and French immigrants who crossed the Atlantic and settled there.

163
The family farm remains a strong component of the culture and the landscape of Nova Scotia, often nestled in amongst the forest.

164

Lush hardwood and boreal forests cover the Cape Breton Highlands, Nova Scotia, in elegant velvety green. The protected lower slopes and moist valley floors are deciduous where the centuries old sugar maple and yellow birch reach the northeast limit of their range.

NATIVE WATERS

FLYING HIGH

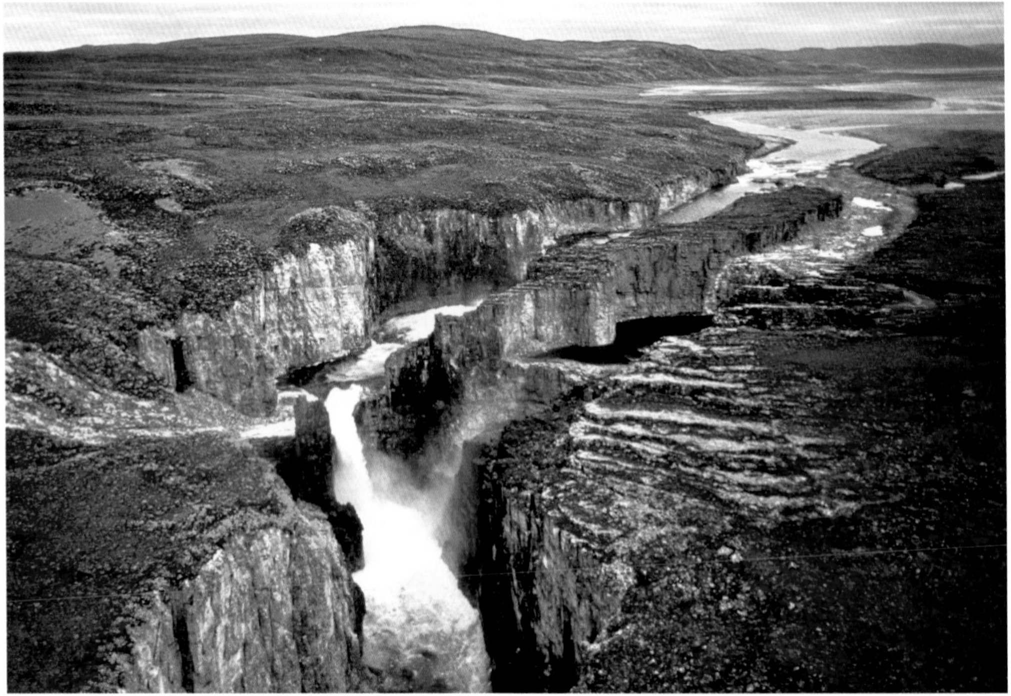

167
Assiniboine River, Manitoba (left); South Nahanni River flows
over the Virginia Falls, Northwest Territories (right).

August is laughing across the sky,
Laughing while paddle, canoe and I,
Drift, drift,
Where the hills uplift
On either side of the current swift.

(E. Pauline Johnson), *The Song My Paddle Sings*

It is not metaphoric to say that the best way to experience Canadian nature is to become submersed in it — jumping right into a glacier lake may be too drastic for some, but getting into a canoe is glorious. A peaceful contemplative drift down the Red Deer River through the Badlands is idyllic. Or try a winding sojourn along the Milk River, whose chocolate-covered waters erode the silt and sandstone banks that crumble and release fossils from their graves, exposing them to the open air and the warm sunshine for the first time in millions of years before they tumble into the water to be buried once again.

The soft banks yield to the demands of the river flow and bend and wind, unable to commit to a straight path. Silently turning a bend, the canoe is met by unsuspecting wildlife drinking at the bank. Lakes bejewel every province and territory in the country — turquoise cupped in a granite setting in the mountains or deep agate green tufted with cattails. The canoe cuts through the mirrored surface that reflects the clouds and trees in a parallel watery paradise. Loons call out their diverse repertoire as celebrated Mohawk Canadian poet Pauline Johnson wrote, "Swelling the song that my paddle sings."

Canada has the largest surface area of freshwater of any other country, with over 30,000 lakes; con-

168
On its journey to the Arctic Ocean from its headwaters in the
tundra of the Northwest Territories, Hood River leaps down
the deep Wilberforce Gorge.

171
The clear arctic waters of this Yukon lake reflect stunning
spectrums of blue when viewed from above.

tributing greatly to the area are the Great Lakes, which in and of themselves hold the honor of the largest freshwater surface area found in any one place in the world. These five grand ponds, fondly referred to as sweet-water seas, are: Lakes Huron, Erie, Superior, Michigan and Ontario, an Iroquois word meaning "beautiful waters." The St. Lawrence River and Seaway is sourced from the Great Lakes, drains into the Gulf of St. Lawrence and then the Atlantic Ocean — an important transportation route. It was a massive project to engineer the channels, locks and canals, yet in most winters the St. Lawrence River completely freezes and closes to shipping, a circumstance no amount of engineering can prevent.

Although much of the freshwater of the arctic is frozen in ice and permafrost, the taiga gushes with unaltered, untamed virginal rivers held in by sheer rock walls rather than manmade dykes. Some of the country's largest waterfalls fall here. High waterfalls and deep canyons characterize Nahanni National Park in the Northwest Territories, cut through by the raging South Nahanni River. Della Falls are the highest in Canada, and Niagara Falls is one of the world's greatest cataracts based on volume.

English settlers were lured over in the early 1900s by the Canadian Pacific Railway to grow the orchards of apples, strawberries, peaches and cherries famous throughout the Okanagan Valley. The Frazer, Skeena, Nass and Columbia rivers irrigate the valley and provide excellent fish habitat. Ospreys nest in the trees and swoop over the waters with their deathly accurate fish-grabbing claws while golden eagles enjoy spectacular aerial views as they follow the paths of the rivers. Kootenay Lake fills the valleys of southern B.C.'s mountains.

The Selkirks and Purcell Mountain ranges can be seen from Kootenay's shore, as can the great Kokanee Glacier. Kootenay or "people of the water" is the name of the First Nations peoples who came to the lake to collect huckleberries and catch salmon.

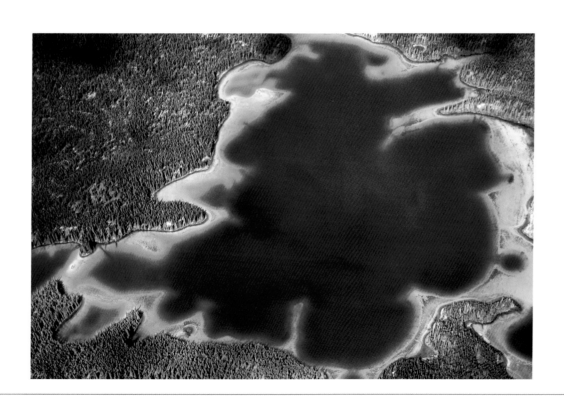

Beautiful Kluane Lake, the largest in the Yukon, drew prospectors with the lure of gold discovery during the gold rush.

Many lakes, waterfalls and rivers have long been mystical places that perpetuate both spiritual beliefs and superstition. The thundering waves against limestone at the Lake Manitoba Narrows create a sound reckoned to be that of the Manitou, or "Great Spirit" in Ojibwa. Legend tells of the old woman who had turned to stone at Parry Falls, while waiting for the hunters to return. Today, the Lutsulk'e people make a pilgrimage to ask the Lady of the Falls where to find the caribou around Great Slave Lake, and she answers by directing the mist from the falls to where they must hunt. Deganaweda was the Iroquois leader, born of the lake, who brought peace from the warring Iroquois tribes, and who removed the monstrous black snakes that filled the waters in legends. Sea monsters are not completely discounted even today, such as Okanagan's mythical Ogopogo, a velative of the Loch Ness monster, or Lake Ontario's finned snake-like Gaasyendietha, first seen by French explorer Jacques Cartier, the first recorded sighting of any sea serpent in North America. The ghosts of the many shipwrecks that occurred on the Great Lakes, which have seen wars and storms of equal violence, continue to haunt the imagination. The Peace-Athabasca Delta, the world's largest delta, at the mouth of the Peace and Athabasca rivers, is a wetland habitat of global significance listed by RAMSAR; it is the habitat for one of the largest populations of wild bison and the nesting grounds of the whooping crane. The world's largest wetland is the Hudson Plains, infamously named "the land of bog and fog." Infested with mosquitoes and black flies, the sloughs and ponds also offer critical breeding, staging and nesting sites for migratory waterfowl using the Central North American flyway. Within Canada's great boreal forest there are few roads and the main means of access is by canoe. Lake of the Woods sprawls over the wooded lands of northwestern Ontario and covets an astonishing 14,542 islands. A canoeist paddling contentedly through this watery landscape, surrounded by fog, mist or rain, experiences a feeling of water everywhere.

FLYING HIGH CANADA

174
The quiet waters of this Yukon lake will soon be frozen into complete winter stillness; the trees are already beginning to show their fall colors.

175
This blue viper has come full circle to catch its tail as it slithers through the forests and ravines of the Yukon.

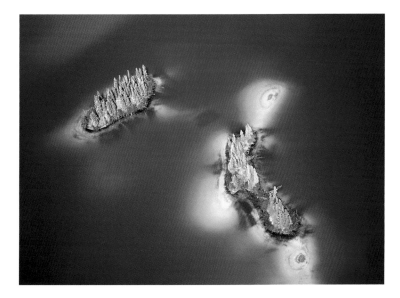

176

The waters of Watson Lake have their blues and greens generously re-
plenished by receiving more annual precipitation than other part of the
Yukon. This moisture also supports lush forests that, in turn, feed a significant timber industry.

177

Small islands wade in the waters of this Yukon lake; those that poke
above the surface are completely covered with trees.

178

A river winds its way through the waterlogged muskeg in the Yukon.

179

The headwaters of the White River are in the Wrangell-St. Elias Mountains and flow into the Yukon transporting rock sediment; this will be taken by the Yukon River, making it brown and silty over much of its length, and deposited into the Bering Sea.

180

Lake Laberge, Yukon, was made famous by Canadian poet Robert Service, who wrote of the derelict boat called the *Alice May* that was set ablaze in poetic style on these cold waters.

181

The clear, clean waters of Coghlan Lake, Yukon, offer a visibility down to 12 m (40 ft) wherein swim abundant lake trout, northern pike and arctic grayling.

182
The tundra and muskeg are saturated with lakes, swamps and rivers in
the Canadian subarctic.

183
Nahanni National Park, in the Northwest Territories, is famed for its beauty and is best observed from a canoe floating down the Nahanni River.

184 and 185
The Nahanni River and the powerful, thundering Virginia Falls
are the most famous spectacles of Nahannni National Park in
the Northwest Territories.

186
Elk Lake Provincial Park is filled with glacial lakes and mountain vistas.

187
Assiniboine Provincial Park, British Columbia, is named for Mount Assiniboine, shown here with Wedgewood Peak surrounded by three glacier lakes, Lake Nagag, Sunburst Lake and Cerulean Lake.

188-189
Glacier-fed lakes such as this arm of Hallam Peak in British Columbia are clean and cold.

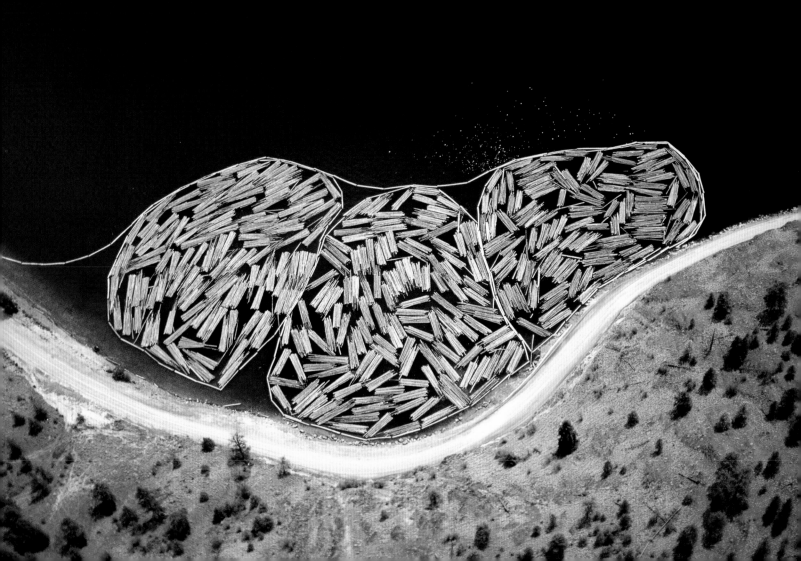

190

Timber logs are lassoed in the waters of Okanagan Lake in British Columbia. Forestry
is one of the most important industries throughout the province.

192

Hector Lake is a glacier lake in Banff National Park, Alberta. The surrounding forest and mountains embellish any hike with fantastic scenery and discoveries.

193

The southern half of the boomerang-shaped Barrier Lake, Alberta, shows the different colors of sedimentation. Prior to the damming of the Kananaskis Valley, no lake existed here.

194
The Athabasca River in Alberta winds through the prairies, boreal forest and muskeg. It is born in the glaciers of Jasper National Park and as a whole is the longest river in Alberta, draining into Lake Athabasca in Wood Buffalo National Park.

195
The rivers, lakes, green rolling foothills and the agricultural crops in the background give a visual summary of a great portion of Alberta's landscape.

196-197
Japer National Park has many blue glacial lakes such as Lake Louise. The montane valleys are sheltered and full of wildlife and the large golf course often finds it-self with as many elk on the course as golfers. There is signifi-cant development in the Jasper townsite, but the surrounding wilderness is biodiverse and pro-tected.

198
The Athabasca River Basin is an intricate system of rivers, tributaries and diversions, running through the great wildernesses of the northern half of Alberta from the Rocky Mountains to the Arctic Ocean.

199
Wood Buffalo National Park is the largest national park in the country and a UNESCO World Heritage Site. Lake Claire is the largest lake in Alberta with an area of 1346 sq. km (520 sq. mi).

200-201

The Athabasca River Valley was first seen by Europeans in the 19th century. It would come to be one of the most important rivers for transport during the fur trade and later be inundated by polluting pulp and paper mills, a problem that persists to present day.

202-203

A forest fire leapt over this river but was exhausted before spreading too far. Fire is a natural and essential component to the health of the boreal forest.

FLYING HIGH CANADA

205
Rivers sprawl almost distractedly through the spectacularly colored tundra landscape
in Nunavut.

206 and 207
A sturdy bridge traverses the Nelson River in Manitoba. The bridge lies
close to the surface of this river whose water level never rises too high
but instead spreads onto a flat floodplain.

208

A tributary of the Assiniboine River, the Little Saskatchewan River
turns tightly at every opportunity
as it winds its way along the lush
treed valley.

209

The fur traders in their birch bark
canoes used to navigate the
bends and turns of the Swan River in Manitoba, encountering
wildlife and native communities
along the route.

FLYING HIGH CANADA

211
Polar bears roam hungrily in search of food. When the waters of Cape Churchill, Manitoba, are frozen, they hunt seals on the ice floes.

212

Lake Erie, one of Ontario's Great Lakes, is the shallowest of the five. It is
shallower than the Niagra Falls are tall, meaning that the lake will even-
tually completely drain when the falls finally erode to the lake's mouth.

213

Lake Ontario, also one of the five Great Lakes, is fed by the Niagara Falls.
It is the smallest in surface area of the five though it exceeds Lake Erie
in volume. It drains into the St. Lawrence River.

214-215
While not outstandingly high, over 168,000 cubic meters (6 million cubic feet) of water fall over the crestline of Niagara Falls every minute, making it the most powerful waterfall in North America.

216
Visitors to Niagara Falls, Ontario, can take a boat ride into the mists of the falls.

217
Three separate waterfalls comprise Niagara Falls: Horseshoe Falls, American Falls and Bridal Veil Falls.

218-219
A little boat of thrill seekers feels the rush of the powerful waters and gets splashed and refreshed by the mists and waves of Niagara Falls, Ontario.

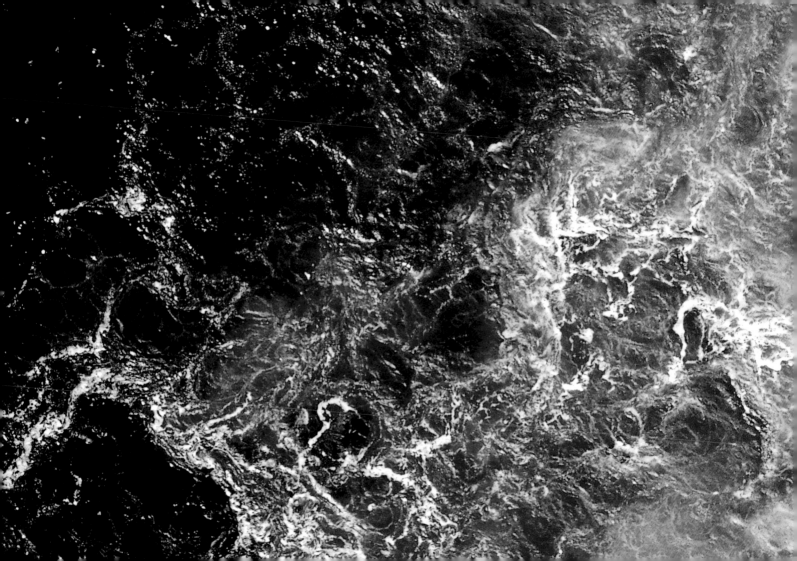

220
A provincial nature reserve is at the mouth of the Montreal River, which flows into Lake Superior.

221
Lake Superior, one of Ontario's Great Lakes, is studded with little tree-covered islands.

222
Little green-treed islands near Silver Islet on Lake Superior, Ontario.

223
Black Bay Peninsula on the north shore of Lake Superior is a remote area with little islands, such as the Burned Islands, that are uninhabited except by moose and birds.

224
Kayakers have found themselves a secluded beach on the shores of
Lake Superior, Ontario.

225
Ships have been docked for the time being on the sandy shores of Lake
Superior, Ontario.

226

The George River forms a great estuary in the Ungava Peninsula of Nunavik, Quebec, that empties into Ungava Bay. The continental ice sheets carved broad rivers and numerous deep dark lakes into this landscape.

227

The Barnoin River flows and falls through the Ungava Barren Lands into Ungava Bay. Sparse vegetation clings to the shallow soils that are sprinkled on the bare rocks in this cold region of Quebec.

228
Salaberry de Valleyfield, south-western Quebec, is an industrial center on the St. Lawrence River.

229
The Coteau-du-Lac National Historic Site has played a major role in the development of river transportation in Canada. It had a lock canal that was a forerunner to the St. Lawrence Seaway.

230
The George River is a historic transportation route that is enjoyed today by recreational canoeists.

231
The geography north of Schefferville, Quebec, is lush and diverse. The abundance of water sustains great forests and grassy plains and supported the hunting and gathering Innu peoples since time immemorial.

232
Water cracks into the shore and extends the reaches of its rivers across the landscape.

233
Low-growing shrubs splash color across the taiga in autumn.

234

Montmagny in southern Quebec was established on the shores of the St. Lawrence river and the mouth of the South River in 1678. The surrounding countryside is primarily farming, dairy and market gardening.

236-237
Musk oxen roam the tundra in the Ungava Peninsula, Quebec. Their thick coats protect them from the cold winds and water cannot penetrate the dense oily wool, even as they wade into these glacial pools in the permafrost.

238-239
Musk oxen, Ungava Peninsula, Quebec. They are often seen in groups of 10 to 20, depending on season and location. In the summer these herbivores may be seen in river valleys, along lake shores and near damp meadows.

240

Caribou migrate across the tundra in spring and fall between breeding, calving and foraging grounds. Often, thousands of animals can be seen traveling together.

241

The George River caribou herd migrates south to their feeding grounds in Northern Labrador and Quebec. They are adeptly aquatic, able to swim across rivers and lakes with ease.

242
The ecoregion of the Long Range Mountains of Newfoundland is covered by sparse coniferous forest, heath and moss and receives abundant snow in winter.

243
The lush wetlands of Labrador are a waterscape of blues and greens.

244

Waterfalls on the Serpentine River in Newfoundland fall in a series of steps to little shallow pools. The water is clean and clear traveling over the rocky bed.

245

A sharp crevasse makes the water leap into a deep gorge before it continues its way through the rocky austere valley.

246
A UNESCO World Heritage Site, the tenth in Canada, Gros Morne National Park protects an area of true Canadian wilderness in Newfoundland.

247
Gros Morne National Park encompasses an area of high mountains extending to the ocean with rivers pouring from ancient lakes and cascading over cliffs thousands of feet high.

248

The St. Croix River of New Brunswick is important both for its stunning biodiversity and its history: some of the first European settlements in the First Nation's territory were built along its banks.

249

McGowan's Corner on Gilbert Island creates a fork in the St. John River, Fredericton, New Brunswick.

250
Yachts and motorboats line the dock at Oromocto marina, New Brunswick.

251
Mactaquac Provincial Park just outside of Fredericton, the capital city of New Brunswick, is full of hiking trails through the woodlands and beaches along the St. John River.

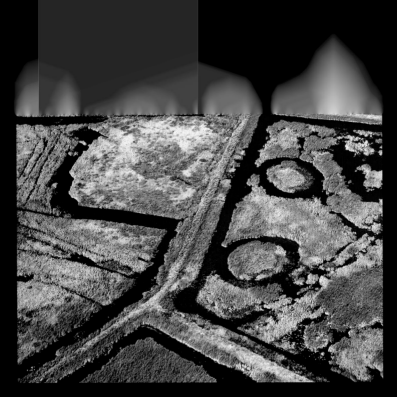

252

Saltwater marshes in the Tintamarre National Wildlife Reserve, on the upper reaches of the Tantramar River, are being restored after years of draining them for agricultural development. Today these marshes are among the densest breeding grounds for many species of birds.

253

There is no clear cut separation between land and sea along the maritime coasts where estuaries and floodplains are common. This river puddles over the coastal landscape irrigating the surrounding farmland.

254-255
A single home is set beside the historic covered bridge over the River Glade in New Brunswick. These relics are routinely monitored with the hope to preserve them. The old wooden structures are weathering but hopefully will remain a part of the river's personality.

256
Saint-Leonard in Madawaska County is serviced by this bridge across the St. John River.

257
New Brunswick is crisscrossed with bridges such as these two examples in Hartland (left) and Upper Kent (right).

258

A covered bridge at Upper Sackville, New Brunswick, is a historical treasure, as these types of wooden bridges are not constructed any more.

259

Old Tracadie Gully, New Brunswick, is full of sand bars and sand dunes
and submerged landscapes.

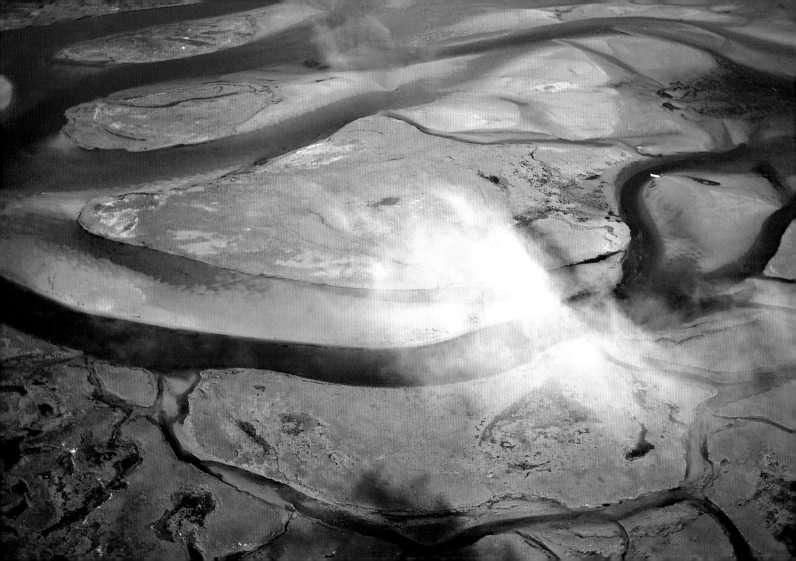

FLYING HIGH CANADA

260
A large rippling sand bar creates intriguing patterns mirroring the ripples of the waters of the St. John River in New Brunswick.

262

Petitcodiac River, New Brunswick, is often referred to as the "chocolate river" owing to its color, created by the heavily silted water. The river exhibits one of the few tidal bores in North America.

263

Located in the Petitcodiac River Valley in southeastern New Brunswick, whose original inhabitants were the Mi'kmaq, Moncton was later settled by the Acadians.

264
A dynamic system of tidal creeks, mudflats and saltmarshes fills the
Cumberland Basin in the Bay of Fundy, New Brunswick.

265
Memramcook River is in the cradle of Acadia in New Brunswick.

266
New Brunswick's famous tides at the Bay of Fundy create floodplains of wetland and mudflats. This is muddy Shepody Bay when the Shepody River runs low.

268
Where the thick forest has been cleared, country houses and agricultural fields are now found around Lake Edward, New Brunswick.

269
Southeast of Fredericton, New Brunswick, Evandale is a small town on the shores of the St. John River. Here, ferries transport the locals to and fro and a boat ride down the river passes little farms surrounded by wildflower fields and woodlands.

270

The Brae River, Prince Edward Island, rolls past a number of communities settled by various immigrant cultures from Europe. The immigrants churches were often built in the architectural styles that prevailed in their homelands. The name Brae is Scottish for "hillside."

271

A red brick church established alongside the water on Prince Edward Island offers a quiet sanctuary for its parish.

272
Flowing parallel to the coastline of New London Bay, French River runs
along the north shore of Prince Edward Island.

273
Farming and fishing communities line the shore of the French River on
Prince Edward Island.

274
Economy River did not get its name for commercial reasons but from the Mi'kmaq word kenomee, which means "a place of land jutting into the sea" and likely referred to the shoreline that protrudes into the Minas Basin, Nova Scotia.

275
Nova Scotia is a land of water, wetlands, marshes, rivers and ocean. The variety of vegetation is as diverse and colorful as the various shapes of land sculpted by these waters.

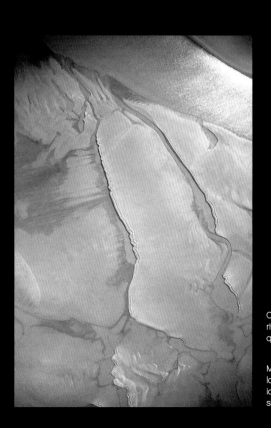

276
Chebogue Point in Nova Scotia when the river is at low tide. The mud here is like quicksand and high tide returns quickly.

277
Mud flats in Debert, Nova Scotia, may look like wastelands but they are ecologically important for invertebrates and shorebirds.

278
The Walton River flows within the Minas Basin watershed, a boggy area full of lakes, coniferous forests and clay plains.

279
The Gaspereau River, Nova Scotia, winds through the valley of the same name and is named after the Gaspereau fish that migrates up the river every spring from the ocean to the freshwater lakes.

FROM HUMBLE FORTS GREW CITIES

FLYING HIGH

FLYING HIGH CANADA

281
View of Toronto (left); and over the St. Lawrence River,
Montreal, Québec (right).

With the soft sun-touch of the yellowing hours
Made lovelier, I see with dreaming eyes,
Even as a dream out of a dream, arise
The bell-tongued city with its glorious towers.

(Archibald Lampman), *The City*

Before there were cities or towns, there were forts, and before that there were only Native villages — and this was not too long ago. The French established the first permanent settlement at Port Royal (now Annapolis Royal) in 1605. Jacques Cartier, the early French explorer, took the Huron word for village, kanata, to call his settlement, which is now part of Quebec City.

Over time "Canada" came to be the name for the entire territory claimed by the British. Forts were established in the early days of the fur trade. Toron-

to now stands on the ashes of Fort York, destroyed by American forces in 1813 but not lost. The Canadian and British troops retaliated by burning the presidential mansion in Washington in 1814, later painted over and forever thereafter called the White House. Rebuilt the next year, Fort York grew into the city of York and subsequently Toronto.

Most forts were established along rivers, the early highways used to cross the expansive wilderness. The numerous river cities are situated on major rivers owing to their early forts, many of which remain preserved as historic parks. The first forts were established on the Hudson Bay, by the Hudson's Bay Company, as gateways to the riches of central Canada. Henry Hudson was an early explorer in the region; one was set adrift in the bay by

282
The B.C. sunshine lights up the façade of the old Hotel
Vancouver, beyond which is the downtown skyline of
Vancouver British Columbia.

285

Parliament Hill, Ottawa Ontario.

his mutinous crew but left behind his name as a legacy. In the coastal subarctic, settlements were established for the fur trade and whaling. Other places were settled for the exploitation of other resources, such as the Yukon for the Klondike gold rush, Edmonton for the oil boom and Uranium City in northwest Saskatchewan, for, obviously, uranium. Some cities were once thriving but now are ghost towns; boom-and-bust is a situation when a town grows exponentially until the resource that brought the people there is depleted and subsequent unemployment forces them to leave. This still occurs within Canada's strongly resource-based economy.

Other towns continue to boom while others seem to hit a stasis and stay small but sustainable communities. There are so many remote towns and villages in Canada that bush planes, float planes, helicopters and dogsleds are well employed. Coastal villages around the Maritimes, Atlantic and Pacific, utilize boats, not cars. Roads do not cut through the thick forests of the northern reaches of many provinces and cars are simply inappropriate in the Arctic. Even the largest towns in the north, such as Yellowknife and Labrador City, have few all-weather roads. The country was first settled in the east and it took some time for populations to cross to the other coast. Montreal was elderly when Vancouver was still virginal rainforest.

The railway already linked U.S. cities, such as Boston and Chicago before the first wagon roads were pushed into interior British Columbia.

The Canadian Pacific Transcontinental Railway forged through the landscape and linked the country from sea to sea. To secure against encroachment from the United States, Canada encouraged immigration by offering the west practically free for the taking. In 1885, a massive migration saw more than 200,000 homesteaders stake their claims. By 1930, half the prairie population was still made up of rural farmers and ranchers.

Today that number has fallen to less than ten percent. However, the ties to the culture prevail and

La Citadelle, in Québec City, is a fortification built under
British rule. The construction of the outer walls began in
1820 and it took 30 years to finish.

cowboy boots and rodeos are still commonplace even in the big business center of Calgary. As patterns shift, and rural people are moving into the cities, so too are the city folk opting to transplant themselves and settle down in the peace and simplicity of a small town. There are few amenities on the west coast islands, such as Salt Spring, Galiano and Pender, but they represent some of the highest real estate values in the country.

Modern city centers are comprised of buildings of brass and glass, with geometric designs of contemporary creativity. Cities, such as Calgary and Toronto, have high pointed towers, making exclamation points on the skylines. Architectural design addresses a climate that buries a city under snow most of the year, ingeniously circumventing the cold by constructing aboveground and underground pedways and tunnels connecting building to building. With heated garages and giant shopping malls that host theatres, amusement parks, hotels and restaurants, in some cities one can pass a Canadian winter without putting on boots or a winter coat.

Owing to the youth of the country, most "historic" buildings date back only a hundred years or so. In addition, because most were constructed of wood, the most readily available building material, many have succumbed to fire and rot. Where history is best preserved is in the green copper-roofed buildings of Ottawa and Old Québec, of strong European influence and flair. Beautiful old buildings endure that were commissioned by the Canadian Pacific Railway company as it forged westward, such as the Banff Springs Hotel and the MacDonald Hotel.

Canadian cities have grown from the collaborations of various cultures whose influences continue to be preserved and celebrated while incorporating the expressions of the new faces that continue to arrive. The cityscape reveals its diversity with mosques, cathedrals and temples and all the other bell-tongued towers.

289
Sunset at Canada Place. This was the venue for the World Expo that Vancouver hosted in 1967; today it is where visiting cruise ships dock.

Vancouver

290

The Burrard bridge and Westside high-rise apartment buildings are in the foreground, beyond which is a view to the forest of Stanley Park.

291

Vancouver is one of the largest, ever-expanding and most popular cities. It has a healthy economy with high business investment, a thriving arts, large parks and beautiful climate.

292-293

Granville Island and the Marina of Vancouver is in continuous growth and development. This photo shows an area that is today mostly high-rise buildings.

294
The evening skyline of downtown Vancouver is elegantly back-dropped by the silhouette of the Coast Mountains.

295
This evening photograph of the Lions Gate Bridge is taken from West Vancouver looking towards downtown.

296 and 297

Calgary is a busy commercial center that has kept its hayseed modesty attired in coyboy hats and boots.

298-299

Deerfoot Trail is an intricate speedway of overpasses linking the sprawling suburbs to downtown Calgary.

300

Edmonton is the capital of the province of Alberta. Established as a fort on the North Saskatchewan River during the fur trade, it is now a government town with a vibrant arts and music scene as well as the home of the University of Alberta.

301

The Alberta Legislature in Edmonton, surrounded by parkland.

302

The most outstanding architecture of downtown Saskatoon, Saskatchewan, is undoubtedly the Delta Bessborough. This city also has a large university campus.

303

This river view of downtown Saskatoon shows the great amount of parkland in the city and the greenbelt that follows the river valley.

Saskatoon

304 and 305

The front gardens of the Provincial Legislative Building in Regina Saskatchewan reach right out to the shores of Wascana Lake. Boasting 34 types of marble in its design, this building was completed in 1912 (both Alberta and Saskatchewan were established in the same year, almost having been designated a single province, and are fondly referred to as "The Buffalo Twins").

306

The merging of the Red River and the Assiniboine River occurs in downtown Winnipeg, Manitoba. From every view over the downtown area the horizon extends onto the wide open prairies.

307

The Pedestrain Bridge over the Red River in Winnipeg, Manitoba, allows pedestrians and bicycles to enjoy the river valley and commute free of traffic.

308 and 309

The Manitoba Legislative Building is surrounded by parkland along the Assiniboine River. The Golden Boy sits at the very top of the Legislative

Hamilton

310

Hamilton, Ontario, is located on the southern shore of the western end of the Niagara Peninsula of Lake Ontario.

311

The Burlington Bay Skyway or Skyway Bridge is part of the Queen Elizabeth Way freeway linking Fort Erie with Toronto. Completed in 1958, it crosses the narrow bar separating Burlington Bay from Lake Ontario.

312 and 313
Downtown Toronto, Ontario, is recognized by the Rogers (sports) Centre, commonly referred to by its former non-commercial name — the Sky-dome, which is the white dome-topped structure below the equally dis-ntinctive CN Tower. The city is established along the shore of Lake On-tario.

Toronto

314-315
This view of the downtown Toronto skyline shows the ever-present CN Tower but this perspective also shows the contrast of the old and the new architecture that blend harmoniously alongside each other.

316
Most of the center of downtown Toronto, Ontario, is brass and glass sky-scrapers except for the distinctly old and elegant Royal York Hotel, front and center in this photograph.

317
Aerial view of Toronto City Hall (the two semi-circular structures to the left), Old City Hall (the brown buildings beside it in the centre) and the Law Courts.

318
The top of the CN Tower gives a bird's-eye view over downtown Toronto
and Lake Ontario.

319
The Skydome, now called the Roger's Center, is the home of Canada's
famed baseball team, the Toronto Blue Jays.

320
Ontario Place in Toronto is a cultural, leisure and entertainment park that
extends over three man-made islands along the Lake Ontario waterfront.
It was inaugurated in May 1971.

321
The harbor and marina on Lake Ontario is close to downtown Toronto,
which sprawls in the background.

323

Toronto, Ontario, by night shows itself as a city that never sleeps. It is a vibrant and important theater city where the lights of Canada's "Broadway" shine brightly.

324
Downtown Ottawa, Ontario, is across the Ottawa River from Hull, Quebec.

325
Ottawa is the capital city of Canada. This photograph of downtown features the Parliament Buildings in front of the Alexandra Bridge (in the foreground) over the Ottawa River. The bridge in the background is the MacDonald-Cartier Bridge.

326
The copper-spired rooftops of the Château Laurier in Ottawa contrast with the rounded rooftops of Canada's Museum of Civilization, across the Ottawa River in Hull, Quebec.

327
Standing majestically on the shore of the Ottawa River are the Parliament Buildings. To the left edge of the photograph is the old Château Laurier (Fairmont Hotel).

328-329
Ottawa, Ontario (left) and Hull, Quebec (right) face each other across the green winding banks of the Ottawa River. Many residents of either city commute between the two for work and recreation. Ottawa is resplendent with old copper-roofed architecture that houses the Parliament Buildings, National Library, Confederation Building and the National Gallery of Canada.

330 left
The National Arts Centre and Skyline of Ottawa at 53 Elgin Street facing the Rideau Canal. The Centre is the largest performing arts center in Canada and hosts performances of music, theater and dance.

330 right
Downtown Ottawa as seen from Elgin Street.

331
The Parliament Buildings. In the foreground is East Block, behind which is Centre Block, the main Parliament building where the House of Commons and Senate chambers are located.

332
Montreal is a culturally diverse and geographically beautiful city.

333
The Jacques Cartier Bridge crosses over the St. Lawrence River in downtown Montreal.

Montreal

334-335
The view from Mount Royal looks to downtown Montreal, Quebec. The circular building is the McGill University McIntyre Medical Sciences Building.

336-337
Downtown Montreal, Quebec, and the St. Lawrence River in the background.

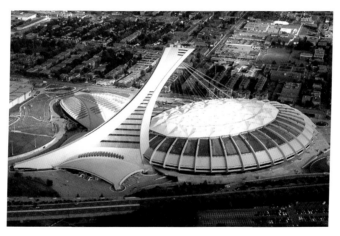

338
Marché Bonsécour (foreground)
and City Hall (background) are
part of the old port of Montreal.

339
Olympic Stadium in Montreal
Quebec.

340
Mary, Queen of the World Cathedral is nestled in the center of this photograph of downtown Montreal, Quebec. The CN building is to its right.

341
In Old Montreal the Notre Dame Basilica takes a central position.

342 and 343
Québec City is the capital of the province with which it shares its name.
Québec City is the only North American fortified city north of Mexico
whose walls still stand and was declared a UNESCO World Heritage Site.

Québec City

344

Three centuries of colonial conquests, a French, English and finally Quebec regime, are at the origins of this unusual architectural aspect.

345

The doors entering Old Québec City, les Portes du Vieux Québec, show the walls of the fortification.

346

Towering above the St. Lawrence River, the Château Frontenac is an historic hotel in Québec City. Charming shops and gourmet restaurants are tucked into buildings dating from the 18th and 19th centuries.

348 and 349

Québec City in winter is a place of festivals, most important of which is
the Carnaval de Quebec, the largest winter carnival in the world. It is a

351

The Plains of Abraham, where the French lost the city to the British in battle. La Citadelle (dating to 1820), built on top of the Cap Diamant, is the eastern flank of Québec City's fortification, in characteristic Vauban style.

352
The Île d'Orléans Bridge is a suspension bridge built in 1940 to cross the
St. Lawrence River between Montmorency Falls, Québec City, and the
Isle of Orleans (Île d'Orléans), a National Historic District (1970).

353
Québec City in winter. A Canadian Coast Guard ice breaker (red & white)
passes through the ice on the frozen St. Lawrence River.

Fredericton

354-355

The St. John River flows in a west-east direction, bisecting the city of Fredericton, the capital of New Brunswick. The river is the dominant natural feature of the municipality and is an important recreational greenbelt with a trail system along both shores for walking, biking and jogging.

356

The Christ Church Cathedral in the green center of this photo of Fredericton is reputed to be one of the finest examples of decorated Gothic architecture in North America, copied from St. Mary's at Snettisham, England.

357

Downtown Fredericton lacks high-rise buildings and instead has several lovely historic buildings along the banks of the St John's River. To the left of the left loop of the freeway is the steepled Fredericton City Hall (1876), the oldest city hall in the Maritimes still in use. The white-domed building close to the first bridge is the Legislative Assembly.

358

Construction of the Legislative Assembly Building in Fredericton began in 1880 and is now representative of Second Empire style, and
looking a bit like a multitiered white-frosted cake.

359

St. Thomas University, Fredericton, New Brunswick, is a small Catholic
institution, dating back to 1910 when it was a boy's school.

360 and 361

Charlottetown's historic waterfront is where the Fathers of Confederation made their historic landing in 1864 and now is where cruise ships regularly make their port of call. The Hillsborough River Watershed is the largest river system in Prince Edward Island.

Charlottetown

362
The Georgian-style Government House of Charlottetown, Prince Edward Island, is the official residence of the Lieutenant Governor of the province and was built in 1834.

363
The same Charlottetown waterfront as the previous page, but in this photo she is wearing her winter coat.

364

Halifax, the capital of Nova Scotia, is where Canada's first permanent British town was established in 1749, on the scenic shores of the world's second largest natural harbor.

365

Halifax Citadel - Fort George National Historic Site had its earliest construction begin in 1761, after the British founded the city in 1749. At noon each day a canon is fired from atop the Citadel.

Halifax

366 and 367

Downtown St. John's, Newfoundland, is along the part of the harbor called the narrows. Cabot Tower on Signal Hill, which is on the left side of the narrows, can just barely be seen.

St. John's

UNDER THE PRAIRIE SKIES

FLYING HIGH

369
The famous prairie fields of gold (left); crops are cut
in intricate patterns, often seemingly artistic (right).

A song of the good green grass!
A song no more of the city streets;
A song of farms—a song of the soil of fields.
(Walt Whitman), *Leaves of Grass*

It's the simplicity, honesty and romance of the prairies that inspires accolades. The sweet-smelling sagegrass prairies and native fescues are home to wild horses and prairie dogs; they are sacred native lands where nature's daytime music buzzes with insects and rattles with snakes, quieting into the starry lullabies of the coyote. Cowboys roam on horseback through their vast cattle ranches and hardworking farmers work a land that feeds the country. The sunburnt face of the landscape smiles skyward, unable to hide its content expression under neither the shelter of trees nor the shade of mountains. The prairie topography is not bold or demonstrative in personality, but it's not shy either; it proudly lays out its colorful acreage as if it were the finest of linens, smooth and elegantly patterned. Agricultural fields are delineated, cut and combed into great coiffured geometrics. The farmland then gradually enhances in color and texture as the seasons mature. Rich brown and organic black soils sprout green and foreshadow the abundance of Canada's breadbasket. Midsummer splendor is a revelry of yellow canola fields, rich green alfalfa, delicate mauve flaxseed and the famous golden wheat fields.

Tireless threshers and combines pace the fields tilling and seeding and finally harvesting and leaving trails of neatly packaged bundles of hay and straw. The lights of lonely tractors are seen late into the

370
Flying over fields and farms on the prairies allows one
to relish a view that extends to infinity.

Under the Prairie Skies

nights of the harvest moons so large and orange on the horizon they seem as overripe as the drooping wheat heads and too heavy to rise into the night sky. Another small light shines like a beacon from the farmhouse where a late dinner is awaiting. Delayed harvest risks ruin in the event of an early frost, which can appear with a snap of Jack Frost's brittle fingers. Like in a winter fairytale the warm Indian summer is instantly cast under an enchanted silvery spell; everything sparkles, the colors subdue into pastels of pink, yellow and blue and the honey-gold sun turns white. Very soon after, the simple prairie dress is luxuriously cloaked in white and the prairie upholds its reputation for cold. Snow is necessary on the prairie, representing most of the annual precipitation that irrigates the vast area of farmland and also sustains some of Canada's most important wetlands. Indeed, there is occasional rain in summer that comes in the form of fantastic thunder-and-lightning storms, events of intense energy and beauty.

Lighting bolts streak across the massive open skies and rains come down hard and fast; the parched land thirstily gulps up the water before the prairie sun and arid winds steal it away. Winds grow unobstructed on the open fields and when different temperaments of wind, cold and hot, approach each other from opposing directions a seemingly territorial battle ensures and they wind themselves up into aggravated frenzies, swirling and churning the ash-gray sky and producing dancing wind funnels and legendary tornados.

The prairies span the provinces of Alberta, Saskatchewan and Manitoba, from the Rockies to the Red River Valley and from the US border north to the aspen parkland that transitions into the great boreal forest. Although an estimated ninety-five percent of the prairies have been turned over into farm and graze lands, the original prairie grasslands survive in rare coveted corners. Perhaps less than one percent of the tall-grass, eighteen percent of the short-grass and twenty-four percent of the mixed-grass prairies remain, and grassland species such as the swift fox

Under the Prairie Skies

and burrowing owl are disappearing. Also disappearing are the old barns and iconic grain elevators. Once located at every town along the railway, grain elevators held the local farmer's grain until the trains passed by to transport it to the large grain terminals at Canadian ports. These sentinels of the prairies were a dominant prairie structure, but are now outdated and, sadly, being torn down one after the other. Similarly, many once-dignified barns and sturdy homesteads now sulk in neglect, abandoned, with sagging moss-covered roofs and paint long faded and peeled away; centennial wooden barns are fast vanishing from Canadian heritage like ghosts without haunts. Other prairie features continue to endure throughout millennia. Not-to-be overlooked gems in this part of the country are the prehistoric Badlands. Contrasting sharply with the surrounding easy gentle expanses, the Badlands are great gorged out valleys filled with fantastical land formations, mushroom-like hoodoos, great rock pillars, sharply chiseled karst spires and countless caves. Sinking into them is tru-

ly stepping back in time as the red, beige, black and terra cotta strata of the canyon walls rise above and the millennia pass in layers of sandstone, clay, shale, mudstone and coal. Eruptions of ridges and buttes, such as Castle Butte, and the spectacular sand dunes of the Great Sand Hills burst up out of the otherwise placid plains.

Dinosaur fossils are in abundance, but the other-worldliness of the scenery would make the appearance of a living, snorting, teeth-gnashing tyrannosaurus contextually applicable. Drumheller, Dinosaur and Grasslands Provincial Parks and the Big Muddy Badlands are chock-a-block with arrowheads, teepee rings, cairns and ceremonial boulders, reminders of their recent ancestral inhabitants. Many stories and events that took place here are lost to the winds and left to the imagination, but moments of refuge for heroes and outlaws, such as Lakota/Sioux Medicine Man Sitting Bull and Butch Cassidy, will be recounted indefinitely. And thus, the romance of the prairie endures.

374
Crops grow right up to the water's edge but for a thin row of trees on this section of the Shuswap River in the B.C. Valley.

375
The fertile British Columbia valleys are warm, sheltered and well-irrigated.

376
An old weathered farmstead still stands on this pioneer farm, reminiscent of an earlier time.

377
A swath of trees is cleared to grow a small crop.

FLYING HIGH CANADA

379
Trees are often considered just another crop and cut and pulped into paper.

380

Feed lots in Alberta are the ugly result of mass production; a brutal contrast to the romance of the traditional ranches.

381

Millions of cows are brought to feedlots in Alberta to fatten up before the

382-383
Small family-run farms still survive
in Alberta.

384-385
Crops are cut in precise lines by this farmer who politely avoids the small swamp area filled in with trees and bushes.

386-387

Harvest time in Alberta is marked
by the tireless work in the fields
and the changing colors of the
leaves on the trees.

388-389

The patchwork of the prairies is
wonderfully colorful.

390

This canola field in Claresholm, Alberta, is a distinct centerpiece in checkerboard of greens.

391

The landscape rolls slightly in Lethbridge, Alberta, and the canola stands out brightly even at a distance.

393
A polka-dot of green on the yellow prairie skirt is likely a small wetland depression where a slough may form in spring; these little wetlands are best left uncultivated.

394

The old red barn, hay stacks, grain silos, a humble country home and possibly a dug out stocked with some trout comprise this classic farmstead in Saskatchewan.

395

The wooded river seems to have lost its way in the cultivated grid and hints at what the land had looked like many years ago.

396
Saskatchewan is famous not only for its farmland, but also for its numerous trout-filled lakes.

397
The Saskatchewan River Basin is an international watershed stretching over the three Prairie Provinces and a portion of Montana.

398
A lush green hayfield in Saskatchewan is being cut and is soon
to be baled.

399
This golden wheat field in
Saskatchewan has just been cut
and will have to be harvested before any rains come in a flash
prairie thunderstorm.

400

Fields are groomed in Saskatchewan in preparation for the next crop. Crops are often planted on rotational basis creating bald and ripe fields side by side. The metal silos store the grains for next year's seed.

402
The topographies of some fields are challenging to cut efficiently.

403
This field in Saskatchewan is being prepared for seeding.

404
This little wooden house is surrounded by a sea of golden wheat that has just been cut.
Next the grains will be collected and the straw baled.

406
The heavy black humus-rich soil of Saskatchewan makes this the most fertile zone in the country.

407
Fields contain various crops side by side and the land is worked in intervals from season to season and year to year. Sections of trees are important buffers and windbreaks.

408 and 409

Grain elevators are the sentinels of the prairies. These stoic beauties are sadly the last of their kind as progress deems them redundant and is tearing them down. The name of the wheat pool and the community was written on the face of each elevator established along the long stretch of the Canadian railway that connected these towns and collected their wheat to transport to central granaries.

410
Sheltered by a wall of trees, this Manitoba farmstead is otherwise surrounded by extensive canola and hay fields.

411
Most of southern Manitoba is cropland. Manitoba is the easternmost of the three prairie provinces.

412-413
Various crops are grown along the shores of Lake Erie, Ontario.

414

A few farming families established in a close community of neighbors work the vast acreage of cropland around them in Waterloo. One enterprise has a livestock facility as well.

415

A simple farmstead in Waterloo has likely been worked by the family for generations, judging by the size of the trees surrounding the farmhouse.

416
The bright red barns and the brick-red house splash some color onto the white winter landscape in Ontario.

417
These barns likely shelter livestock that is fed by the grain stored in the tall silos on this sturdy self-sufficient farm in Ontario.

419

Ontario farmland covered in an even layer of smooth snow reflects the soft winter sunshine in shimmering pastels.

FLYING HIGH CANADA

420
A small Ontario farm near Fullerton, Ontario, is sparsely sheltered from the winter winds which can blow fiercely across the flat open fields.

422
A fertile valley in Saint-Omer, in the Baie-des-Chaleurs, Quebec.

423
The picturesque Bas-Saint-Laurent region extends east along the St. Lawrence River from the little town of La Pocatière to the village of Sainte-Luce and is particularly fertile agricultural land that employs almost a third of the regional labor.

424-425
Small farms and communities build up along the rivers in Quebec.

426
The area near Dalhousie Junction, New Brunswick, are naturally forested hillsides except for small clearings made for agricultural purposes.

427
Quebec is not often compared to the highly productive prairie provinces, but agriculture is a large sector of this province's economy.

428-429
New Brunswick has a diverse landscape that also includes small sections of cropland.

430-431
Many hands make lighter work, in the hot dusty days of summer in New Brunswick.

432
An exclamation point of water punctuates its surprise at being completely surrounded by denuded land (New Brunswick).

433
Canoeing and kayaking down the Tobique River, New Brunswick, takes one on a winding sojourn past forest and field.

434
Perfectly groomed fields lie behind this little farm near Lake Edward in New Brunswick.

435
A thin dirt road bisects the fields in Grand Falls, New Brunswick.

436-437
A lonely tractor works the fields late into the afternoon in Ortonville, New Brunswick.

438 and 439
Both the fields and the leaves of the trees are a mosaic of red and green
in the autumn in Nova Scotia.

440
The peaceful serenity of a church is accentuated by the soft colors of the countryside and the lofty lazy clouds on the horizon.

441
The forest seems to be trying to win back its land as it encroaches from either side of this cultivated valley, northeast of Margaree River, Nova Scotia.

442
The mild Atlantic climes are well-suited for agriculture on Prince Edward
Island.

443
The forests and the fields commingle and mature in the early fall on
Prince Edward Island.

444 and 445
These quiet little farmsteads have the benefit of both flat fertile farmland
and fantastic oceanfront views (Prince Edward Island).

448
Preparing the brick-red soil in Prince Edward Island for seeding.

449
A single tree remains standing in this cultivated field, perhaps guarding the crop.

450-451
Several species of bird benefit from following the tractors working the field owing to the insects that get turned up from the soil.

452
A small patch of cropland in Mount Hope, Prince Edward Island, surrounded by forest.

453
A creative checkerboard of green and red on this farm in Kirkane, Prince
Edward Island.

454
Traditionally, people living the remote isolated farming life sought out the sense of community that can be found with a church parish. A small country church such as this one would bring farming people together once a week on a much needed day of rest.

455
Wheat fields are also a part of the Maritime landscape near Indian River, Prince Edward Island.

456

Anne of Green Gables is a little red-headed girl who won the hearts of Canadians and has become somewhat of a legend. This is her home in Cavendish, Prince Edward Island.

457

A little farm in Kildare, Prince Edward Island, with its sturdy barn, productive crop and little vegetable garden, shows a scene of picture-perfect country living.

FLYING HIGH CANADA

459
The fields of green and red have all turned a snowy white and the tractors are silent and left to slumber through the quiet frosty winter.

460-461
These cows and horses must be kept fed, sheltered and warm through a long Canadian winter.

462 and 463
The snow falls clean and smooth on the flat country fields, the shadows of the trees cast long across the plains, and the winter air is crisp and clear, setting the eyes upon a view that stretches endlessly toward the horizon. These are the images of winter in the countryside of Prince Edward Island.

AN ARTIST'S PALETTE
FLYING HIGH

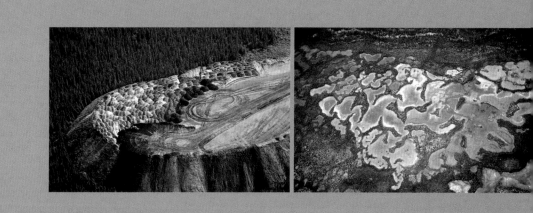

FLYING HIGH CANADA

Dressed in robes of gorgeous hue
Brown and gold with crimson blent
The forest to the waters blue
Its own enchanting tints has lent

(Susanna Moodie), *Indian Summer*

Man has long strived to replicate the colors, textures and scenes of nature onto canvas. We have all been inspired to either pick up a paintbrush or a camera and capture some moment or composition that has impressed us. Yet, no reproductions can ever match living color. The intensity of fire, the subtlety of light, the magic of water and purity of color is captured only by the mastery of Nature herself. The sights are breathtaking in natural wonder. The landscape is painted with abstractions beyond the skill of civilization's most celebrated artists. So definite in hue and tone, the adjectives used to describe a color are actually nouns: terra cotta, jade, sulfur, aquamarine.... Nature's palette requires no mixing or blending, the colors are sincere, not contrived. Millennia of boiling and compressing organics and inorganics have passed to create the colors and textures that amaze and impress us. Minerals lend vibrant hues to the landscape, layered boldly in ancient strata or poured onto the scene in volcanic outbursts. Our appreciation for Nature's creations has become somewhat fanatical and in lust for these attractive rocks and minerals, industry has cracked open the landscape, chopped the tops off of mountains and scratched great scars that bleed royal blue, crimson or even chartreuse. Our standards of beauty have made certain rocks and stones something more than they really are and have made us desire what no other animal would find use for...a dia-

469

The Slave River basin, Alberta.

470-471 and 472-473

A water treatment plant and eastern shores, New Brunswick.

mond does not nourish, gold does not offer shelter. However, along with other precious and semiprecious stones, they are important industries in Canada. Sometimes the colors poured onto the landscape are offensive, garish and sickly from chemical mixtures that would never occur in nature but that are the signature strokes of mankind's excesses. Mining and extraction of elements such as iron ore and sulfur create abstract images such as red lakes or yellow mountains. Some minerals do serve us, however, such as coal and oil. Canada is rich in fossil fuels, the burning of which is an addiction that we are only in the first stages of trying to kick. The tar sands are a huge project in northern Alberta where machines dig up, transport and process the oily soil nonstop, twenty-four hours per day. The resultant moonscape is an eyesore, but while we remain unwilling to implement alternatives, these resources will be exploited to exhaustion. Water is a manipulator of color, reflecting and refracting light to trick our eyes. Rivers act like chemists mixing and churning sediments into brilliant concoctions. Glacier rivers carry fine glacier-eroded sediment, called glacier flour or rock flour, that is dumped into glacier lakes creating a lovely powdery blue-gray color and often a banded pattern to the water. Delta's spill onto flat terrain and splashes of blue and green stain the fabric of the land. Fens and bogs create ribbed and striped patterns of vegetation and water. Salt marshes and estuaries pull colorful minerals out of the ground they lie on, painting the water and the shores surprising colors. Mudflats are sculptures of shape and texture. With every change in tide, there is a new picture to view; each tidal collage admired but for a brief moment in time before it is brushed off the slate by a wash of waves. The sun, wind and rain all affect Nature's canvas, continuing to morph it and manipulate it. Fog and frost create surreal ghostly scenes and sparkling electric definition. Each blow of wind scatters leaves and ripples the waters and sands on an ever-changing screen. Humidity and light further accentuate the colors. These images are forever works in progress, and though captured in these photographic moments, living art can never be framed.

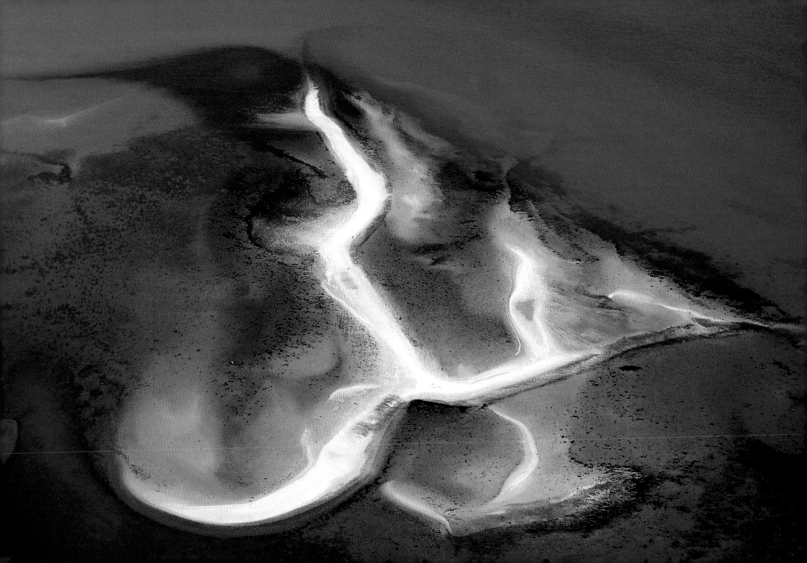

474
Aerial images of sand and water in Quebec show scenes of places that are
otherwise unseen and surely unvisited.

475
The floodplain of Lower Wedgeport, Nova Scotia, has veins like a leaf where the
water tries to find direction.

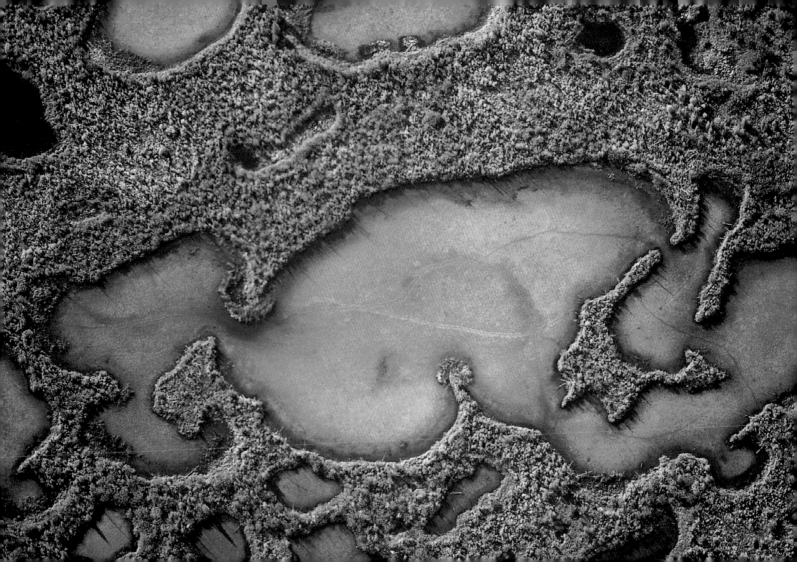

476
Algae and minerals cause the waters of Great Slave Lake, in the North-west Territories, to appear anything but blue.

477
The extensive wetlands of Great Slave Lake make the Northwest Territories one of the most important habitats for birds and other wetland species in North America.

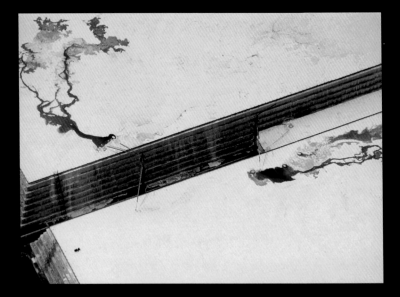

478
Copious amounts of sulfur are extracted from the earth at the infamous Alberta
Tar Sands.

479
The landscape in Fort McMurray, Alberta, is unearthly from the heavy extractive
practices at the Tar Sands.

480-481
The bright red soil in northern Quebec is high in iron content, and the mining of iron ore is an important industry in Quebec. Canada is the world's third largest iron ore producer, behind Australia and Brazil, and approximately 95 percent of that comes from Quebec and Labrador. This is the now-closed Schefferville Iron Ore Mine in northern Quebec.

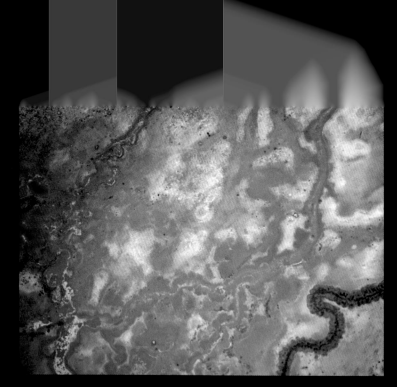

482 and 483

One of the most fascinating features in Wood Buffalo National Park, Alberta, are the salt marshes. Underground springs lift and deposit the salt and other minerals, painting colorful mosaics on the plains. Salt-rich marshes provide excellent habitat for bison, many birds and unique plants accustomed to salt-rich water. These marshes serve as a unique reminder of a time when this area was salty ocean.

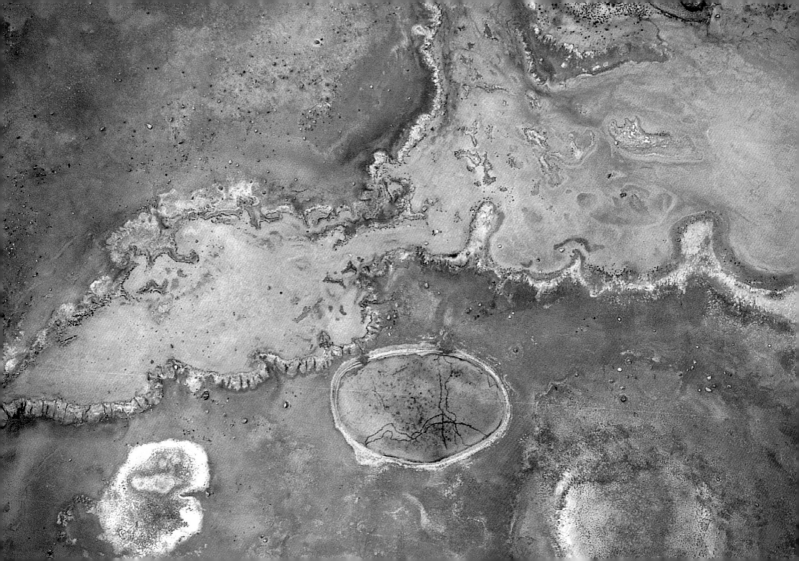

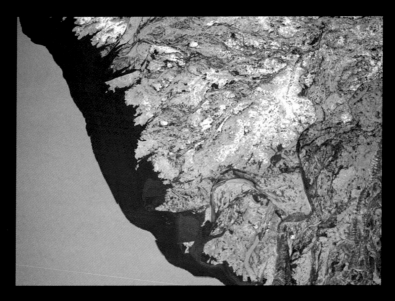

484 and 485

Alberta's tar sands, also known as oil sands, are bitumen deposits; viscous oil that go through heavy treatment to convert it into an upgraded crude oil that can then be used in refineries to produce gasoline and other fuels.

486-487

Bright hematite is mined and concentrated at the Scully Mine at Wabush, Labrador. For 40 years, the Iron Ore Company of Canada discharged up to 23 million tons of fine grained waste rock (mine tailing) into Wabush Lake. The red hue covered over 20 km (12 mi) of the lake.

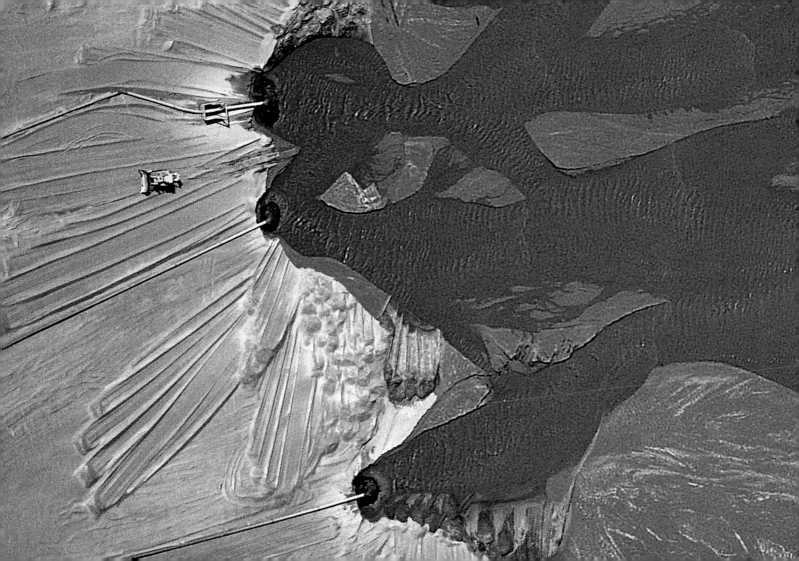

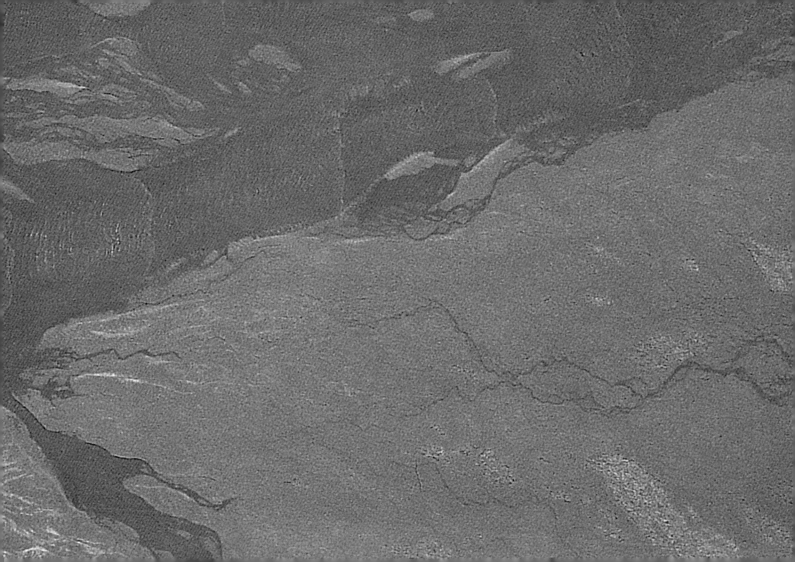

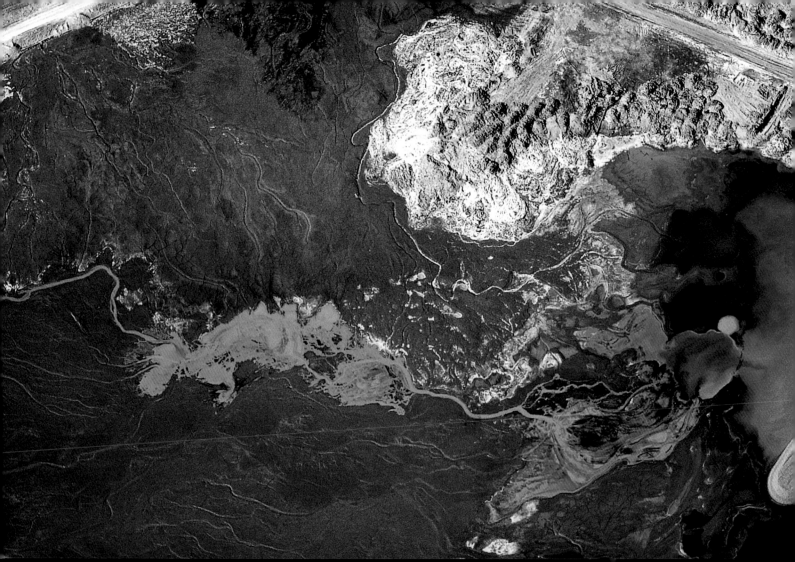

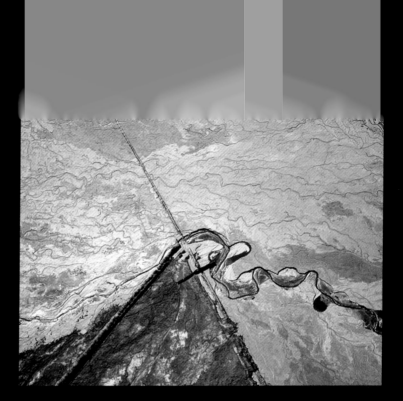

488 and 489

Named after the famous South African diamond mine, the town of Kimberly was founded on mining.

490-491

Canada is mineral rich, creating mosaics of color on the landscape.

492-493

Cape Jourimain is a National Wildlife area. The most common ecotype protected is marshland -- primarily saltmarsh, freshwater marsh and brackish marsh along with extensive sand dunes, which make for intriguing aerial views of color and texture.

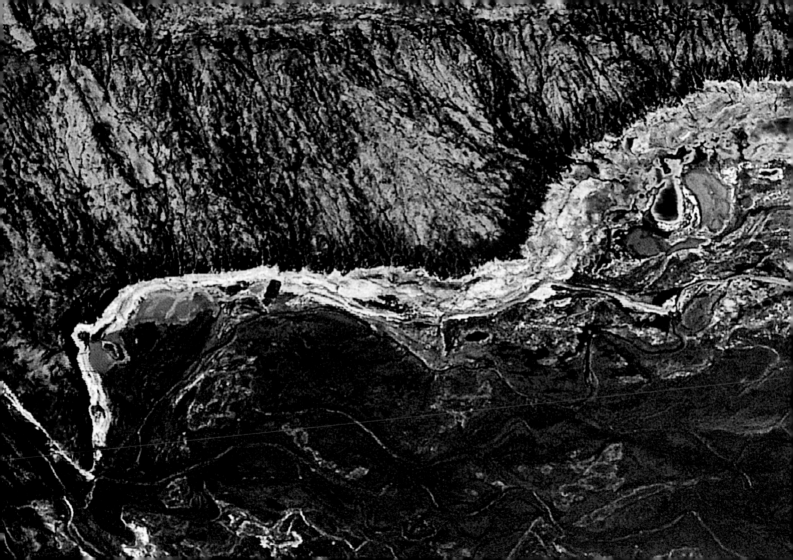

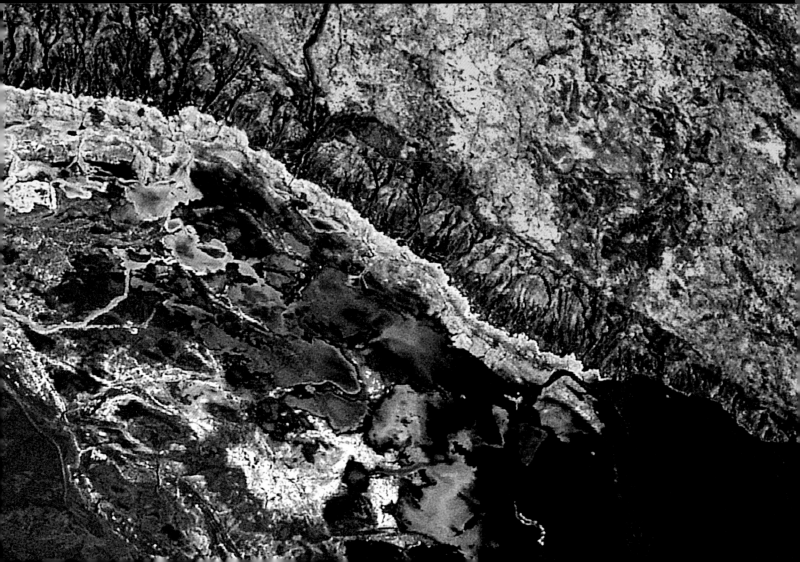

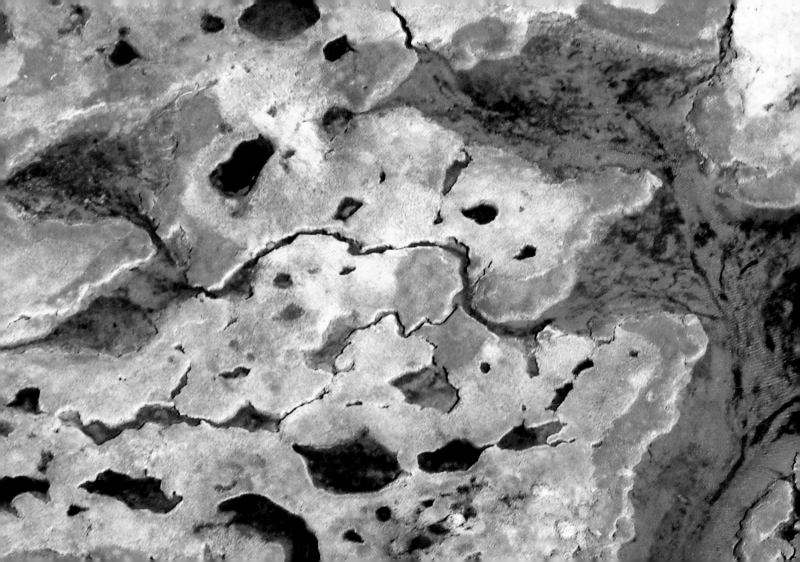

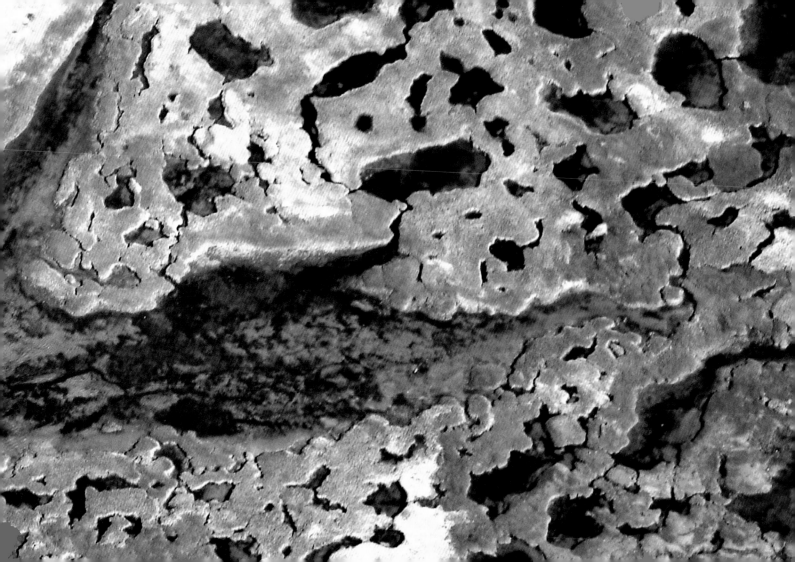

495

The tides at the Bay of Fundy, New Brunswick, leave glistening sand banks and mudflats — spectacular scenes that change with every new tide.

496-497

Sackville, New Brunswick, is on the western fringe of the Tantramar Marshes, tidal wetlands partially transformed to farmland by dykes first built by the original Acadians in the 17th century. The marshes remain one of the largest tidal wetlands in the world.

498-499

A wastewater treatment plant in British Columbia tries to find a way to contain and clean contaminated water.

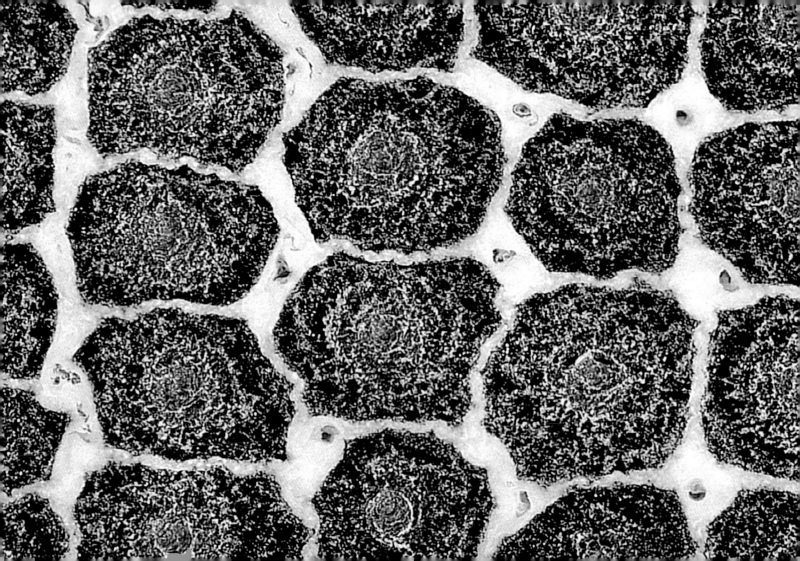

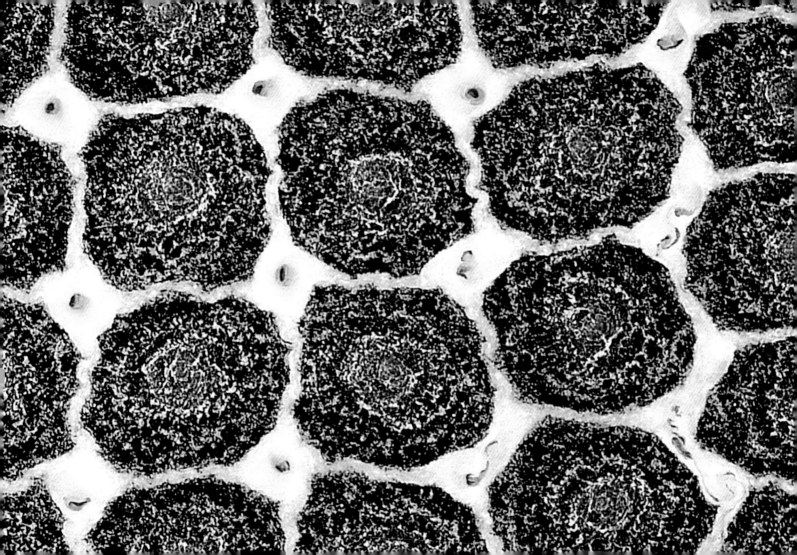

FLYING HIGH CANADA

501
Water takes to the air in the form of fog, reflecting light and shadow and hiding entire forests at Lake Superior, Ontario.

ATLANTIC & PACIFIC COASTAL BOOKENDS

FLYING HIGH

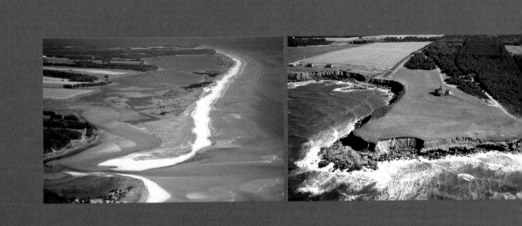

Not long ago there was no land to be seen. Then there was a little thing on the ocean. The rest was all open sea. Raven sat upon this little thing. "Become dust!" he said, and it became the Earth.

Haida creation legend

The west coast of Canada is rich in native legend and mythology, where the orca, the eagle, the salmon and the raven are revered. The Haida and Tlingit, who were taught by the raven how to build the canoe, navigated and fished the jagged coastlines and erected the iconic totem poles that still reach skyward telling their ancient legends to the winds. The "People of the Totem" have been living on the west coast and Haida Gwaii (the Queen Charlotte Islands) for thousands of years. Their dugout canoes now share the waters with huge cargo ships, sailboats, motor boats, fishing vessels and ferries. Compared to the booming southern coast of British Columbia, the northern coast and islands are quite wild; pods of killer whales are frequently seen, grizzlies congregate during the salmon runs in almost clichéd images of wild Canada and bald eagles seem to outnumber humans. The B.C. coast is part of the Pacific Ring of Fire, a narrow, semicircular area known for volcanic eruptions, hotsprings and earthquakes. The waters of B.C. lack sea ice and the climate boasts the most temperate in Canada.

The coast is rocky, jagged and mountainous with abundant islands, deeply indented bays and tidal inlets, an inland sea at the Strait of Georgia, numerous sounds, such as Puget Sound, lagoons, es-

504
Newfoundland's Cape St. Mary is a famous avian sanctuary
where thousands of sea birds, such as gannets and puffins,
line the cliffs with their nests.

507
The islands and peninsulas of Prince Edward Island take on a
new persona when covered in snow than from the colorful
summer personality.

tuaries, saltwater marshes, straights and fjords; the deepest fiord in the world is Findlayson Channel, with soundings of over 795 m (2608 ft). The west coast trail on Vancouver Island is the most famous, expensive and exclusive in Canada. Its fame is owing to its raw and natural beauty, which requires 70 ladders, 130 bridges and four cable cars to connect the 75 km (47 mi) of trail.

Atlantic Canada, comprised of Labrador and Newfoundland with the three maritime provinces of Nova Scotia, New Brunswick and Prince Edward Island, is unique both geographically and culturally — right down to the accent. Maritimers are of Scottish, Irish, English and Acadian heritage, and their Celtic fiddling and step-dancing rivals that of the motherland. The native peoples are the Mi'kmaqs and Maliseet. Lighthouses are abundant to guide boats through the famous dense fog patches that permeate the island-studded waters.

Lobster traps and fishing nets litter the beaches where fishing has been a way of life for the Mar-

itimers for 400 years. Cabot Trail on Cape Breton Island, the little fishing village at Peggy's Cove in Nova Scotia and the Halifax Harbor where docks the *Bluenose II*, the replica of the famous schooner on the Canadian dime, are a few of Atlantic Canada's coastal celebrities.

The mainland coast of Nova Scotia and most of the Bay of Fundy are essentially ice-free. Red sandstone cliffs and hard volcanic rocks tower over wide beaches with great sand dunes and world-record tidal bores topping 15 m (50 ft). Beyond the shallow Grand Banks and the Scotian Shelf, the Atlantic is defined by deep water with icebergs the size of small mountains, mostly underwater and feared by sailors for centuries who named the stretch of ocean from Greenland to southern Newfoundland "Iceberg Alley."

However, the Atlantic and Pacific coasts represent a minority of total Canadian marine coastline. Two-thirds of Canadian coast is splashed upon by the Arctic Ocean. Canada's is the longest coastline

White silica sand beaches are found at Basin Head, Prince
Edward Island. These sands create a unique squeaking
humming sound when walked upon.

of any country in the world, thanks to its numerous fjords, inlets and islands.

The only land border is with the United States to the south and the politically disjunct state of Alaska to the west. From sea to sea, coastal diversity is remarkable. High island endemism includes examples such as the Vancouver Island Marmot, the blond "Kermodei" bear, a subspecies of black bear, and the Roosevelt elk.

Estuaries and fiords provide critical habitat for countless migrating shorebirds and waterfowl, such as the trumpeter swan and sandhill crane. Steep, rocky coastal cliffs provide ideal habitat for some of the largest seabird colonies in the world on the islands of the Atlantic, namely the Gannet and Funk Islands. Upsurges of marine currents in the Arctic Ocean create the ice-free polynyas where cold nutrient-rich waters provide the habitat for narwhal, bowhead whales and walruses.

Polar bears roam the coastline and icebergs hunting seal; thousands of harp seals raise their beautiful snow-white pups on the ice. Though the Arctic and its inhabitants seem hardy and resilient, in truth they are exquisitely delicate and many are endangered.

The great migration of the gray whale is celebrated from Alaska to Baja California but has disappeared from the Atlantic after centuries of hunting. With frighteningly dramatic rises in global temperatures, the freshwater ice caps are being swallowed by the ocean's salty thirst, in turn causing sea levels to rise and feast on the coastline habitats.

The Grand Banks are among the most biologically productive marine areas in the world but overexploitation by national and international fishing fleets nearly wiped out Canada's northern cod stocks and by 1992 was under moratorium. There are fears the once-rich Grand Banks cod may never again support a commercial fishery. However, the tides may still change, by listening to and respecting the voices of the whales, wolves, bears ... and of course, the Raven.

FLYING HIGH CANADA

510
The thickly wooded inlet of Nimmo Bay tucked into the far northern B.C. coast is a fisherman's dream location.

511
Abundant wildlife exists in this diverse habitat of ocean, forest, mountains, tidal pools, rocky cliffs, inlets and sheltered bays.

512
The beacon from this lighthouse warns boats of the rocky uninhabited coast of the Queen Charlotte Islands/Haida Gwaii where barely another light shines.

513
The salmon fishing off the northern B.C. coasts brings fishermen from far
and wide.

514
The rocky shore of west Vancouver Island faces unobstructed out to the
Pacific Ocean taking the full brunt of winds and waves as evidenced by
the bare rocks and wind beaten trees.

515
Trees of the temperate rainforest on the coast of British Columbia grow
right up to and onto the rocky shoreline.

516 and 517
Cape Churchill in Manitoba is where the ice first forms along the western coast of Hudson Bay. Polar bears roam the coast waiting for the water to freeze over to then hunt for seals on the ice floes.

518 and 519 left

The wreck of the *MV Ithica*, once owned by Mussolini, lies stranded and rusted off the coast of the Hudson Bay. In September 1961, the ship was caught in a wind storm while shipping nickel from Rankin Inlet to Montreal and pulled onto the tidal flats where it has remained ever since. It can be reached on foot during low tides and when Hudson Bay is frozen over.

519 right

Legendary storms in the Great Lakes and Hudson Bay caused many shipwrecks such as this one, grounded since 1960.

520 and 521

Fort Churchill, Hudson Bay, Manitoba, dates back to 1717, but was never fully completed. It had four bastions and the curtain walls mount forty-two cannons. Initiated by the Hudson Bay Company it was originally called the "Churchill River Post." In 1719, the post was renamed Prince of Wales Fort.

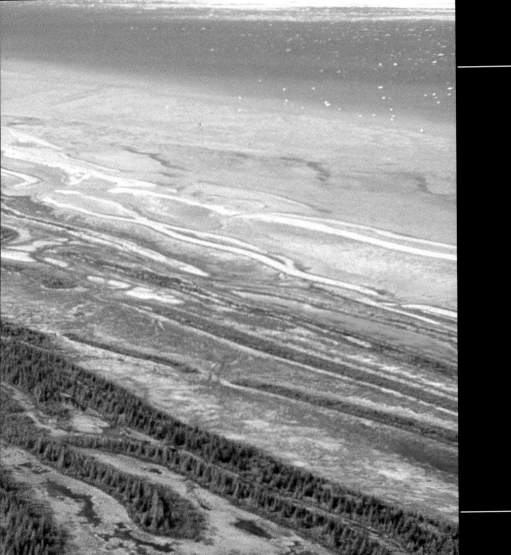

522-523
The James Bay lowlands form the Quebec and Ontario shore of James Bay. The lowlands are a vast wilderness area of taiga/boreal forest where most of the communities are First Nations. Few roads exist but the famous railway is called the Polar Bear Express.

524
Forillon National Park is noted for its awesome coast, which falls abruptly to the water at the tip of Cap Gaspe, the edge of which is guarded by a lighthouse.

525
The little village and marine estuary on the coast of Saint-Fabien-sur-Mer, Quebec.

526 and 527
The Iles-de-la-Madeleine (Quebec) are a long and narrow group of barrier islands in the Gulf of St. Lawrence accessible only by boat or plane. A few thousand Madelinots, descendants of French Acadians who settled here in the 1500s, inhabit the quaint wooden houses, few of which lack a view of the steel-blue waters.

528
A prim white border delineates the property of this lighthouse keeper on
one of the remote coastal fringes of the Iles-de-la-Madeleine, Quebec.

529
Fishing is the primary economy of the population on the Iles-de-la-
Madeleine, Quebec.

530
Cap Bon Ami is within the Forillon National Park, Quebec, established in 1971.

531
Percé is a small historical fishing village on the tip of the Gaspé Peninsula, Quebec. The Mi'kmaq people lived off the sea here for centuries and subsequently the Europeans came and established their fishing community.

532-533
White and red lighthouses are the sentinels of Quebec's jagged shore, warning ships of the shallow rocky waters that surround the land.

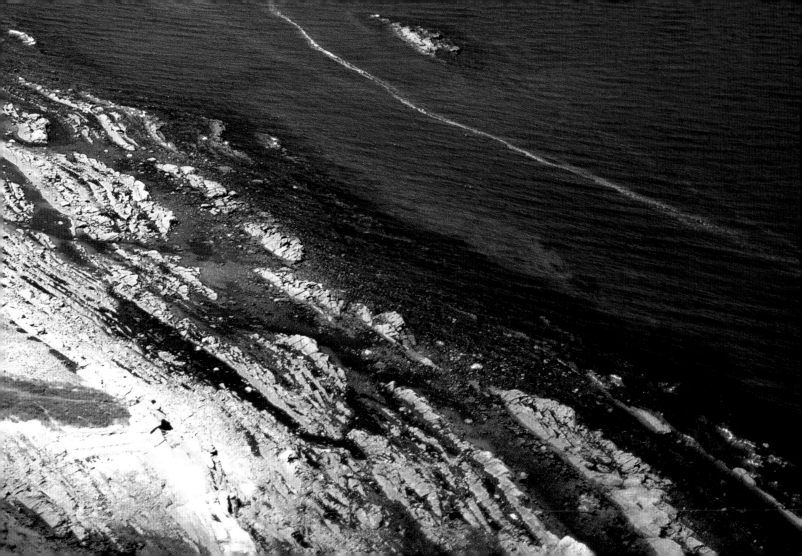

534 and 535
The Sacred Islands — Great Sacred Island and Little Sacred Island — lie in front of Sacred Bay in Newfoundland. The rocky shores are to be respected, a reminder made by this wreck that rusts on the rocks of Great Sacred Island.

536
This fabulously deep fjord is found along the Labrador coast.

537
There is a small town at Barge Bay, south-east of Goose Bay in Labrador, and a large amount of green forested coastline.

FLYING HIGH CANADA

538
The coastal cliffs of the Torngat Mountains on the Labrador Peninsula are billions of years old. The name is an Inuktitut word meaning "land of spirits."

539
The lighthouse on Quirpon Island, northwest Newfoundland, was established to guide ships through the treacherous Strait of Belle Isle, an important shipping route between Canada and Europe in the early 20th century.

540

Murray Beach Provincial Park, New Brunswick, is located along the Northumberland Straight, and is a popular camping area where one can wake up to see the sunrise from out of the ocean.

541

St. Andrews by the Sea, New Brunswick, is Canada's first seaside resort town. It is now home to many prominent families and has been designated a National Historic District.

542 and 543 right

Old Tracadie Gully, New Brunswick, is a natural channel created by a gap in the coastal barrier dunes.

543 left

Low flatlands create broad estuaries that become separated from the Gulf of St. Lawrence by a series of lagoons and coastal dunes of transported sediment. Gaps in the dunes create coastal rivers and channels and barrier islands.

544
Forty little cottages host visitors to Parc de Aboiteau and its lovely coast, on the southeast shore of New Brunswick.

545
The Miscou Island Lighthouse, as well as Shippagan and Black Point lighthouses, are special features on the scenic coast of this island.

546 and 547

Fish farming is a growing industry in the Maritimes. These examples in
the waters of New Brunswick show enclosure's for fish that are raised
captive but in the natural ocean waters.

548-549
Lush greenery right up to the sandy beaches in New Brunswick.

FLYING HIGH CANADA

551
Two kayaks dip their noses into the surf, ready to explore the shoreline of Richibucto, New Brunswick. There is abundant shoreline to explore with plenty of sandy beaches for gentle banking.

552

Low sand bars rippling into the blue ocean waters, backed by fields of green, create swirls of color that inspired this piece of New Brunswick's coast to be called Peacock Point.

553 left

Accessible only by passenger ferry, Heron Island is an island gem of New Brunswick.

553 right

The sandy shores and cliffs at Shemogue Head, New Brunswick, suffer erosion from the relentless waves and tides.

554 and 555
The constant movement by wind and water of the fine sand causes this 2000-year-old dune, which extends 12 km (7.5 mi) into Bouctouche Bay, New Brunswick, to continuously change shape. The extensive board-walk helps to protect this rare ecosystem.

556
An old lighthouse watches over Cape Enrage, in Albert County, New Brunswick, and the pounding tides in the Bay of Fundy.

557
This abandoned lighthouse on Grindstone Island dates to 1859 and is on the Endangered List of the New Brunswick Lighthouse Society.

FLYING HIGH CANADA

558
St. Croix Island is a small uninhabited island near the mouth of the Saint Croix River that forms the international boundary between Main and New Brunswick. It was neutral territory during the war of 1812 and is now an International Historic Site.

560 and 561
Confederation Bridge connects Borden-Carleton, Prince Edward Island, to Cape Jourimain, New Brunswick. It is the longest (13 km / 8 mi) bridge over ice-covered waters in the world; this photo is in summer when the waters are ice-free.

562
Prince Edward Island National Park features sand dunes and sandstone cliffs, barrier islands, sandy beaches and sand pits. In 1998, Greenwich Peninsula was added to the park to protect the unique dune formations and the associated flora and fauna as well as archeological findings.

563
Watercolor creations are painted on the landscape at Amherst Cove, Prince Edward Island.

564

Point Prim Lighthouse on Prince Edward Island was built in 1846 and is still active. This red and white brick tower is the oldest lighthouse on the island and the only round brick lighthouse in Canada.

565

Lighthouses come in all shapes, sizes, colors and settings on Prince Edward Island. There is a society established to protect this important component of the local cultural heritage.

566
Prince Edward Island has many beautiful areas of coastline that have few houses and ample scenery.

567
Red Point with its white sand beaches is a popular real estate section of Prince Edward Island.

568
A little shore cottage has its boat temporarily dry docked (Tignish, P.E.I.).

569
The caboose of an old train has been parked in this field to spend its retirement as a small coastal dwelling (Cablehead, P.E.I.).

570
Cousin's Shore on Prince Edward Island is a beach area that is undergoing sand dune restoration.

571
Cape Tryon 2 was constructed in 1969 and is still active. It is an endangered lighthouse for its precarious position near the edge of a seriously eroded cliff. The relocated original Cape Tryon dates to 1905 and is now a private residence.

572
Cottages and farmhouses dot the coastal countryside of Lower Darnley, on Prince Edward Island.

573
Prince Edward Island's Cavendish Beach is a popular recreational beach owing to its fine sand and attractive dunes.

575

Chéticamp is an Acadian community on the west coast of Cape Breton Island, Nova Scotia, on the famous Cabot Trail.

576

The Acadian Mountains create rolling vistas right up to the shores of Nova Scotia. Cape Smokey is actually a popular ski hill, a rarity in the Maritimes.

577 left

In the 1930s the first road crossing the rugged Cape Breton Highlands of Nova Scotia was completed and named after the famed explorer John Cabot, who led the first Europeans to arrive on Cape Breton in 1497.

577 right

St. Ann's Bay is nestled along the Cabot Trail in Cape Breton, Nova Scotia. There are many artisans and craftsmen with galleries in this region.

578 and 579
The Three Sisters Mountains at Lake O'Law are striking geologic formations.

580 and 581

Kejimkujik National Park is one of the least disturbed shorelines of Nova Scotia's southern coast. Brackish ponds, broad tidal flats, white-sand beaches, salt lagoons, secluded coves, and a salt marsh characterize this tundra-like coastal woodland of dense scrub alder and sheep laurel.

LAND OF THE MIDNIGHT SUN

FLYING HIGH

583
Snow in the Arctic can take many forms and textures (left).
Deep and wide fjords along the coast of Baffin Island (right).

I walked on the ice of the sea
Wondering I heard
The song of the sea
And the great sighing
Of new formed ice

(Uvavnuk), *Igloolik Inuit poem*

Crashing calving icebergs, massive glaciers, floating icecaps mimicking true terra firma, so much of the Arctic is adrift and in motion. This icy land is fluid, plastic, ever-morphing. Waterways between islands freeze into frigid ice bridges in winter and break apart in spring; pathways across the ice change continuously. Arctic coastlines extend and retreat as the ice builds and melts. Winds whip up the snow like the sands of the desert. Mountainous peaks and towering crests of ice and snow warp, break and rebuild. Further south, even the land undulates with the great seasonal migration of thousands of porcupine barren-ground caribou crossing the tundra between the summer calving grounds in the north and the winter ranges in the taiga forest. The Arctic is the most sparsely populated region of Canada and where four out of five inhabitants are Inuit. The howling wind and moaning cracking ice have more prevalent voices in the far north than people. Cars are non-existent, and Canadians living here are likely to commute by skidoo or dog sled. As the majority of the Canadian population crams huddled, as if for warmth, along the country's southernmost border, the Arctic to them is most often not only on the periphery of geography but also on the periphery of thought; yet, approximately forty percent of the nation's total land mass is Arctic and two-thirds of the marine coastline is along the Arctic Ocean. Together

584
The tips of icebergs do not reveal the mountain
that is below water.

587
In deep winter the water freezes over and can be crossed by dogsled.

588-589
Great caribou migrations across the tundra of the Northwest Territories.

with Greenland, the Canadian Arctic Islands comprise the world's largest, and as yet unnamed, archipelago, which includes Baffin Bay and the Hudson Bay, a great flooded glacier depression, and is bookended by the Beaufort and Labrador Seas. Early mariners were lured to the frigid Arctic waters in search of the northern route to the Orient. The names of the islands recount the nations who explored this region: Victoria, Sverdrup and Queen Elizabeth Islands, Norwegian Bay and Prince Edward Sound. The Canadian Arctic is representative of one-fifth of the world's total Arctic ecosystems; the northern tip of Canada is 768 km (477 mi) from the North Pole and true magnetic north is within Nunavut's political boundaries. The far north is the land of the midnight sun in summer and a dawnless moon in winter. A polar winter's night is measured in weeks rather than hours; daylight is the soft blue light of the moon reflecting off the snow. When the sun first comes out of hiding, it rises and sets in the south only briefly peeking over the horizon. Glacial ice of the Laurentide Ice Sheet blanketed northern Canada near the beginning of the Pleistocene epoch two million years ago and massive glaciers have scoured over these lands at least four times. The last glaciers retreated from the tundra 8500 years ago leaving a trail of moraine and erratic, torn up from the underlying Canadian Shield of granite bedrock. Chunks of glacier ice broke and created lakes. Permafrost, frozen water-logged soil, reaches depths of 450 m (1476 ft). Long eskers look like claw marks from a giant prehistoric cat rather than a glacier that scratched its way across the terrain. Repeat freeze-thaw cycles sculpt the landscape with patterns and make hummocks heave and active mud "boil." The southern Arctic is not the archetypal frigid mass of ice and snow but a stunningly diverse and beautiful region. Muskeg transition south into open treeless tundra meadows that are roamed by musk oxen and tundra wolves and are resplendent with Arctic wildflowers in spring, followed by the hatching of billions of insects in summer. But, it is the High Arctic where the imagination travels and where the polar bear remains the monarch of an icy domain. Indeed, the Greeks called this region *Arktikós*, country of the great bear.

FLYING HIGH CANADA

FLYING HIGH CANADA —

591
The great caribou herds that migrated across the plains of what is today called the Northwest Territories were followed by tundra wolves and nomadic native communities for centuries, long before Canada was a country. Today, some herds, such as this one, eleven thousand strong, are privately owned.

592
Devon Island, the largest uninhabited island on Earth. The flat-topped plateau is an old erosional surface and characterizes the island.

593
Melting glaciers can form lakes on top of themselves in the Northwest Territories.

594-595
Cornwallis Island lacks any large peaks or ice caps, is low lying and has few bluffs and hills.

596

Two female harp seals with their pups float on sheets of pack ice. The white fur of the pups camouflages them against the snow. Seals are hunted for their fur for clothing, meat for food and fat for fuel. They are also the main prey of the polar bear.

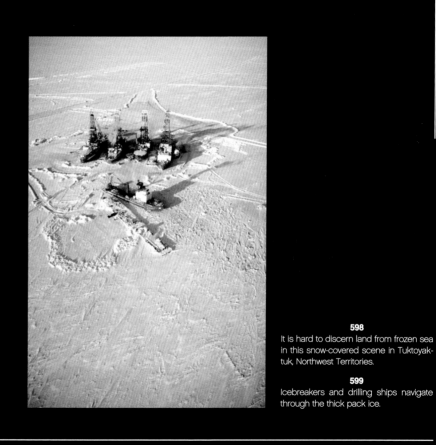

598
It is hard to discern land from frozen sea in this snow-covered scene in Tuktoyaktuk, Northwest Territories.

599
Icebreakers and drilling ships navigate through the thick pack ice.

600
A bulldozer pulls carts over frozen Wellington Channel to transport supplies to a team searching for a wreck under the ice.

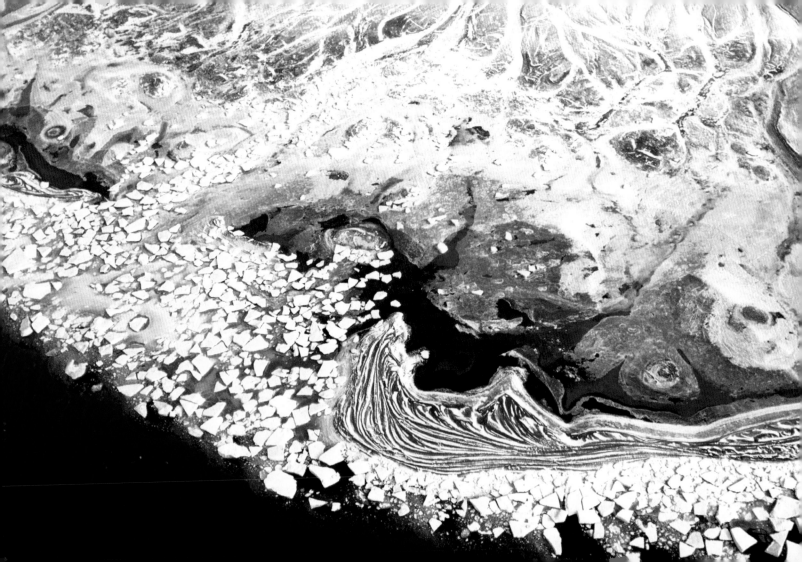

602
Devon Island in the Arctic Archipelago is a polar desert in the High Arctic.

603
The coastal areas of Devon Island are steep sea cliffs. A substantial ice cap, remnant of the Laurentide/Inuitian ice sheet, still occupies the easternmost third of the island.

FLYING HIGH CANADA

605
The Mackenzie Delta in winter becomes crystalline. The patches of snow on the flat bare Canadian Shield are interspersed with patches of conifers and a winding river.

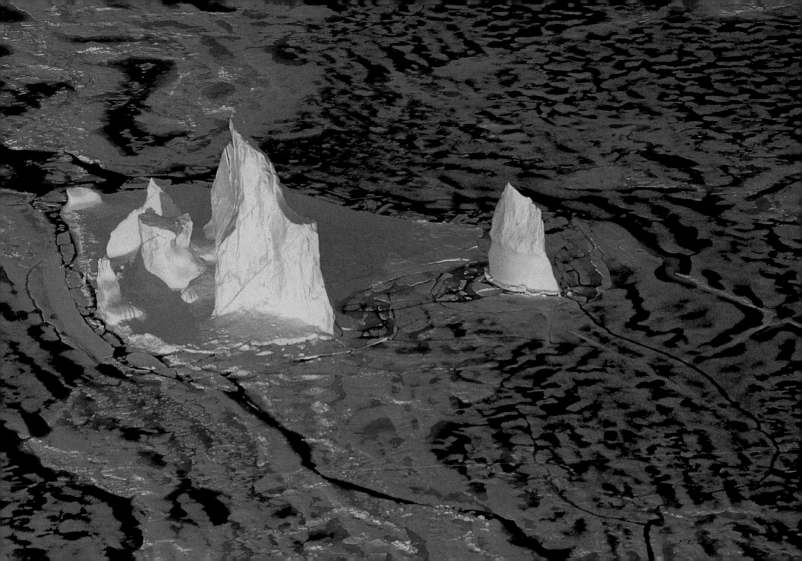

606
The delicate twilight accents the sculpted ice at the tips of these icebergs. The cool blue tone of the iceberg underwater highlights how much more of this mass is hidden from sight.

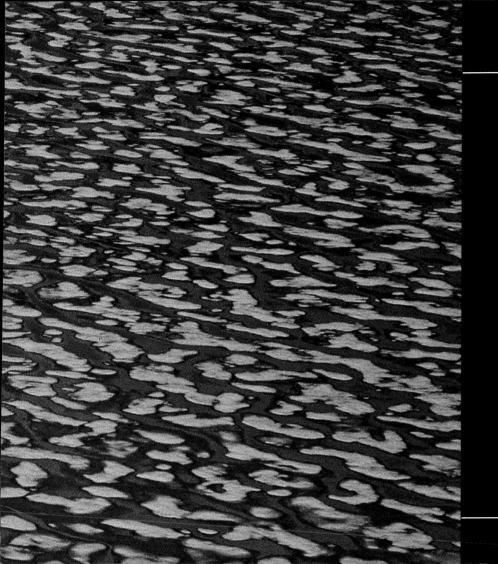

608-609
Although this iceberg is of significant size, what is seen above the surface of the water accounts for about a mere 10% of the entire mass.

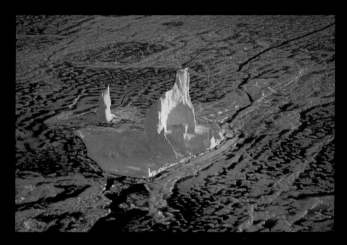

610
As the pack ice breaks up in spring it disengages and becomes ice floes.

611
This iceberg is melting into a creative ice cave; soon it will completely disappear into the salty Arctic waters.

FLYING HIGH CANADA

613
Intriguing layered patterns appear as the ice freezes and cracks on the surface of a lake on Baffin Island. Water remains frozen much of the year but small fluctuations in temperature and humidity play with the plasticity of the ice.

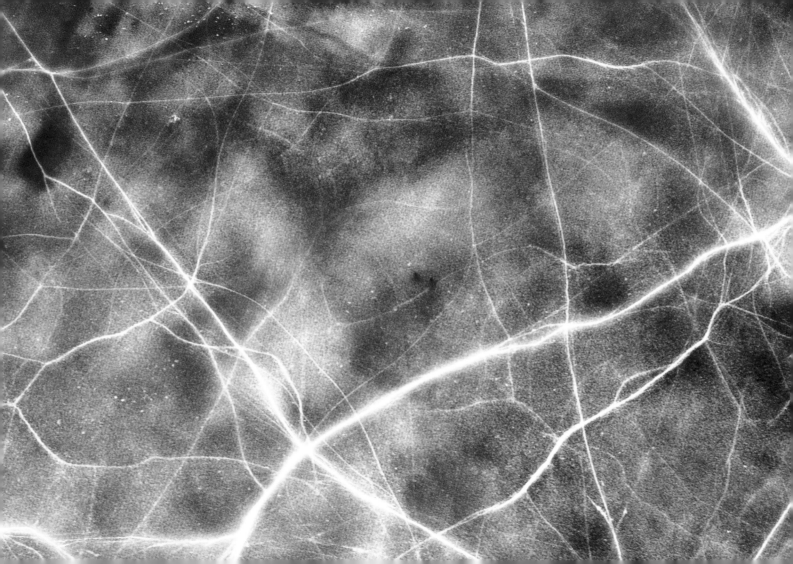

614
The spectrum of color is limited in the High Arctic, but the intensity of blue and white more than compensates.

615
Most of Nunavut is within the Arctic Archipelago, comprised of many un-inhabited islands surrounded by ever-changing horizons of icebergs.

616

The Hudson Bay from above is almost purely enveloped in white on this day with snow and fog almost completely cloaking the mountains.

617

The Hudson Bay was the epicenter of the fur trade when boats and sleds came from all directions to sell and trade their wares. It is still today, hundreds of years later, a remote place and not a place one would imagine having been a great commercial center.

618
Sea meets sky and snow mirrors cloud in the Arctic.

619
The Inuit have ancient knowledge as how to navigate through
this vast whiteness.

620

Icebergs are dangerous things to boats and expertise is needed to safely navigate Arctic waters.

621

Like pieces of a puzzle, once interlocked icebergs break and drift apart. These floating ice sculptures can be as large as city blocks and even those that appear relatively small are deceptive because up to 90% of their mass is below water.

FLYING HIGH CANADA

623
The tightly compressed ice has trapped air pockets that scatter light in such a way that it registers blue to the human eye, when in fact, no color pigment exists in this frozen water.

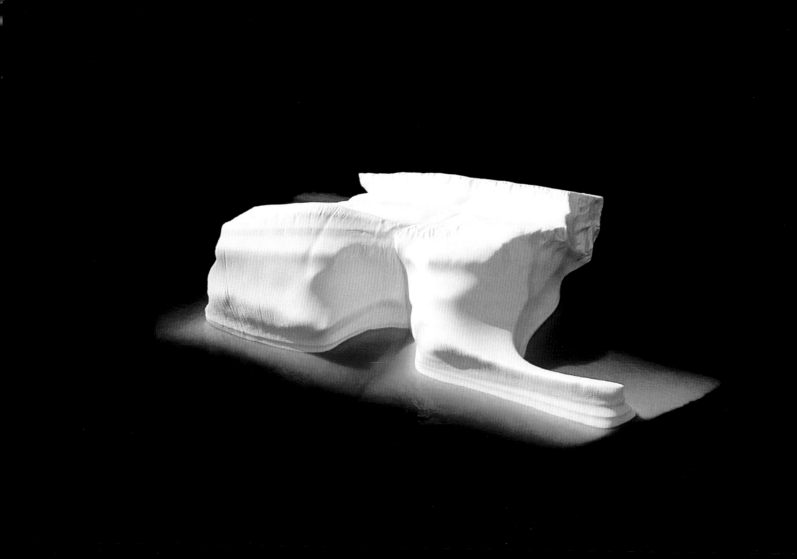

624 and 625
Works of art, the stunning ice sculptures captured in these photos have long since melted into the sea.

627

A moonscape of snow, much of the Arctic is uninhabited and unexplored. This icy up-heaval accents the otherwise flat and topographically featureless terrain.

628-629

The mountains along the northeast coast of Baffin Island receive light snowfall but are capped by ice and segued by glaciers.

630-631

The steep coastal mountains of the Pangnirtung Fjord are reflected in the still, clear blue waters.

Index

Index

Index

Erin McCloskey was born in 1970 in Edmonton, Canada. She took her degree in Conservation Biology at the University of Alberta, eager to pursue her driving commitment to the protection of the planet's environment and ecology. She has furthered this goal as an editor and writer for publishers and conservation organizations specializing in publications and projects on environmental, ecological, scientific, health & lifestyle, geo-cultural, and eco-tourism topics. She published *Hawaii from the Air* (2003) and *Ireland Flying High* (2005) with White Star Publishers.

Photo credits

Sibylle Allgaier: page 175; Theo Allofs/zefa/Corbis: page 174; Yann Arthus-Bertrand/Corbis: pages 110 right, 136, 137, 140, 141, 142, 143, 338, 340, 341, 344, 346, 592, 594-595, 602, 603; Marcello Bertinetti/Archivio White Star: pages 40, 112, 583 left, 614, 615, 616, 617, 618, 619; Alberto Biscaro/Masterfile/Sie: pages 292-293; Dean Conger/Corbis: pages 94-95, 96, 98, 99; W. Perry Conway/Corbis: page 596; Gordon Fisher/Agefotostock/Marka: page 149; Larry Fisher/Masterfile/Sie: pages 298-299; John Foster/Mastefile/Sie: page 627; Fridmar Damm/zefa/Corbis: page 82; José Fuste Raga/Agefotostock/Contrasto: cover, page 83; Ron Garnett: back cover, pages 2-3, 4-5, 8, 9, 18, 28-29, 30-31, 50, 51, 54-55, 60-61, 63, 67, 72, 73, 75, 76-77, 81, 84, 85, 86, 90-91, 92, 104, 105, 117, 124-125, 127, 132, 134-135, 138, 139, 152, 153, 154-155, 160, 161, 162, 163, 164, 167 left, 168, 180, 181, 182, 183, 188-189, 190, 193, 205, 208, 209, 228, 229, 232, 233, 234, 248, 249, 250, 251, 252, 253, 254-255, 256, 257 left and right, 258, 259, 260, 262, 263, 264, 265, 266, 268, 269, 270, 271, 272, 273, 274, 275, 276, 278, 279, 281 left and right, 285, 287, 296, 297, 300, 301, 302, 303, 304, 305, 306, 307, 308, 309, 312, 317, 318, 319, 321, 324, 325, 327, 328-329, 336-337, 339, 342, 343, 348, 349, 351, 352, 353, 354-355, 356, 357, 358, 359, 360, 361, 362, 363, 364, 365, 366, 367, 369 left and right, 370, 374, 375, 380, 382-383, 384-385, 386-387, 395, 396, 397, 406, 407, 408, 409, 410, 411, 422, 423, 424-425, 426, 427, 428-429, 430-431, 432, 433, 434, 435, 436-437, 438, 439, 440, 441, 442, 443, 446, 447, 448, 449, 450-451, 452, 453, 455, 459, 460-461, 462, 463, 472-473, 474, 475, 492-493, 495, 496-497, 503 left, 504, 507, 508, 524, 525, 527, 530, 531, 532-533, 540, 541, 542, 543 left, 544, 548-549, 551, 552, 553 left and right, 554, 555, 557, 558, 560, 561, 562, 563, 564, 565 left, 566, 567, 570, 571, 572, 573, 575, 576, 577 left and right, 578, 579, 580, 581, 588-589, 620, 632, 640; Lowell Georgia/Corbis: pages 591, 598, 599, 605; Ed Grifford/Masterfile/Sie: pages 289; Pat O'Hara/Corbis: page 187; Peter Johnson/Corbis: page 212; Kit Kittle/Corbis: page 158; Kord.com/Agefotostock/Marka: pages 334-335; Dan Lamont/Corbis: pages 120, 121; James Leynse/Corbis: page 323; Randy Lincks/Masterfile/Sie: page 35 right; Gunter Marx Photography/Corbis: pages 35 left, 78, 79, 118, 119, 186, 295, 514; Gail Mooney/Masterfile/Sie: page 291; Christopher J. Morris/Corbis: page 123; P. Narayan/Agefotostock/Marka: page 316; Paul Nopper: pages 12-13, 16-17, 26, 44-45, 46-47, 49, 52-53, 100, 101, 102, 103, 133, 236-237, 238-239, 240, 241, 310, 311, 332, 333, 522-523, 583 right, 584, 587, 606, 608-609, 610, 611, 613, 621 right, 628-629, 630-631, 633, 634-635; Albert Normandin/Masterfile/Sie: pages 282, 290; Neil Rabinowitz/Corbis: pages 510, 512, 513, 515; Joel W. Rogers/Corbis: page 511; Galen Rowel/Corbis: page 593; Alan Schein Photography/Corbis: page 313; Alan Sirulnikoff/Agefotostock/Marka: page 294; Vince Streano/Corbis: page 114; Scott Tysick/Masterfile/Sie: page 320; Jim Wark: pages 1, 6-7, 10, 11, 14-15, 32-33, 39, 42, 43, 56, 57, 58, 59, 64, 65, 66, 68-69, 70-71, 80, 87, 88, 89, 93, 106, 107, 108-109, 110 left, 128-129, 130, 144, 145, 146, 147, 150-151, 156, 157, 167 right, 171, 173, 176, 177, 178, 179, 184, 185, 192, 194, 195, 196-197, 198, 199, 200-201, 202-203, 206, 207, 211, 213, 214-215, 216, 217, 218-219, 220, 221, 222, 223, 224, 225, 226, 227, 230, 231, 242, 243, 244, 245, 246, 247, 277, 376, 377, 379, 381, 388-389, 390, 391, 393, 394, 398, 399, 400, 402, 403, 404, 412-413, 414, 415, 416, 417, 419, 420, 444, 445, 454, 456, 457, 465 left and right, 466, 469, 470-471, 476, 477, 478, 479, 480-481, 482, 483, 486-487, 488, 489, 490-491, 498-499, 501, 503 right, 516, 517, 518, 519 left and right, 520, 521, 526, 528, 529, 534, 535, 536, 537, 538, 539, 543 right, 545, 546, 547, 556, 565 right, 568, 569, 621 left, 623, 624, 625; Ron Watts/Corbis: page 36; Karl Weatherly/Corbis: page 74; Nik Wheeler/Corbis: page 345; Ralph White/Corbis: page 600; Jeremy Woodhouse/Masterfile/Sie: pages 314-315, 326, 330 left and right, 331; Michael S. Yamashita/Corbis: page 62

© 2006 WHITE STAR S.P.A.
Via Candido Sassone, 22-24
13100 Vercelli - Italy
WWW.WHITESTAR.IT

ISBN-10: 88-544-0175-7
ISBN 13: 978-88-544-0175-4

REPRINTS: 1 2 3 4 5 6   10 09 08 07 06

Printed in Thailand
Color separation: Chiaroscuro and Mycrom, Turin

640

Grand Manan Island in the Bay of Fundy, New Brunswick, has high cliffs and rugged scenery that attracts artists and writers. The sheltered Dark Harbour sustains a unique dulse (edible seaweed) industry.

FLYING HIGH